An Overview Series Publication

Database Fundamentals

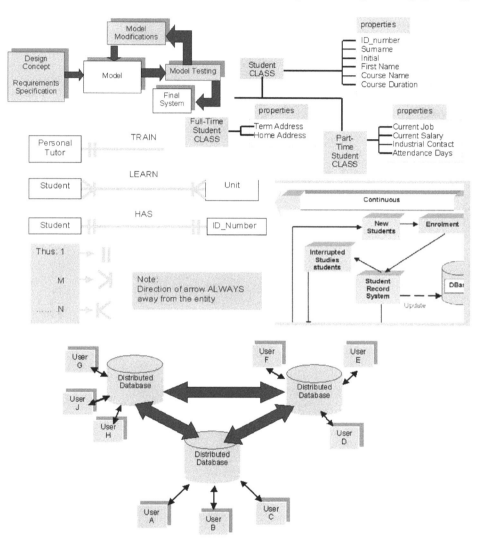

Dr. Goran I Bezanov PhD

published by MIG Consulting Ltd

This page is intentionally left blank

DATABASE FUNDAMENTALS

AN OVERVIEW SERIES PUBLICATION

By Goran Bezanov PhD

Published by
MIG Consulting Ltd
31 Vicarage Road, London SW14 8RZ

British Library Cataloguing in Publication Data
A catalogue record for this book is available from the British Library

International Standard Book Number: 978-0-9558153-3-1

To my Sons
Ognen and Milos

This page is intentionally left blank

PREFACE

This text is a very brief overview of database systems. My aim was to write a text that can be read and understood by readers who are not overly familiar with modern database development techniques. It was my intention that, from this text they could gain sufficient understanding in order to know where to look for further direction. I cover briefly topics relating to general database design and implementation with examples of typical solutions using Microsoft Access database. Briefly the chapter contents are as follows.

Chapter 1 introduces the subject of databases and provides an overview of database systems and functions that are typically supported by database management systems. A brief discussion of database types and design issues such as data dependence, redundancy and anomalies is also provided.

Chapter 2 considers the subject of data modelling. Here a brief description of the different model types is given, but the main emphasis is on Entity Relationship Diagrams (ERD) that are commonly used in relational database design applications.

Chapter 3 introduces the Microsoft Access database and provides a brief glimpse of the features that are supported. Emphasis is on providing sufficient information to enable the reader to begin using the database.

Chapter 4 offers an insight into aspects of database design. These include database normalisation and also the methods used in defining tables, attributes and relationships in database design.

Chapter 5 gives a brief overview of project management. This covers the general aspects of planning and organising development projects. Here requirements specification is described in a general sense. The chapter is therefore useful not just for databases but also for general project management in a technical discipline.

Chapter 6 offers an example case study of a typical approach towards organising and implementing a database design project. Here the stages of development are listed and each of them is described in relation to a typical database design project.

The text ends with an appendix, which provides an example solution to the case study described in Chapter 6. This is intended as an example of the structure of the documentation that accompanies a typical solution to a database project.

My special thanks goes to Borislav Benak for his contribution towards the solution to the library database problem discussed in Chapter 6 and also for the documentation provided as technical documentation in the appendix.

This is my first draft and I shall revise and correct the errors in the next. Suggestions welcome to: mig@consultant.com

Thank you

Goran Bezanov (September 2008, London)

Contents

CHAPTER 1 DATABASES

1.1. Introduction to database systems

Electronic database systems have been used for many years in business and commerce as well as engineering to store data so that it can be processed to provide users with the information that they need. A database is a software program that stores information, which relates to a particular activity or purpose. There are many different activities that require a database to store information. For example, a bank needs to store the information relating to customer accounts, a hospital needs to keep data about patients and the medication dispensed, a university needs to maintain a record of it students, an Internet sales business needs to track orders and payments and many more examples. Data can be financial to describe a volume of sales, or it can be telemetered data from a control system to show the performance of a machine. For example, formula 1 racing teams use real-time monitoring of performance, and analyse this in order to improve performance of their machine.

A database includes tools to help organise and maintain the data. [1,2,3] A database design engineer must know and be able to use these tools in order to make the database efficient and accurate. For example, suppose the phone numbers of students in a university are stored in various locations: in a card file containing student phone numbers, in examination information files in a file cabinet, and in a spreadsheet containing finance information. If a student's phone number changes, it will be necessary to update that information in all the places. In a properly designed database, the information is updated once and all other occurrences of this within the database will be updated automatically. Thus, a principal requirement of any database system is the ability to generate, store and retrieve data efficiently. The basic components of typical database systems are shown in Figure 1.1. Here data is stored in electronic form that allows it to be modified, stored and retrieved. The inputting of data can be automated such as reading data electronically from sensing equipment, or human operators can input it. [4] Before data can be truly useful to the end user, it must be processed so that it yields information.

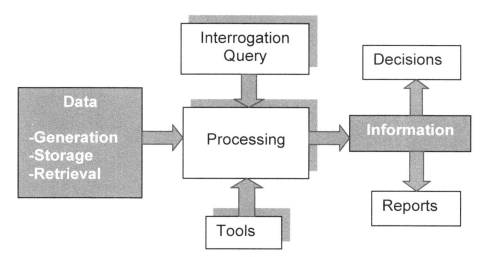

Figure 1.1 Basic components of a database system

For example, you may need a database to store information about students that are enrolled in a university. These databases are very common and they are usually referred to as student record systems (SRS). If for example, you wanted information about a particular student it would be possible to print on the screen all the student data and look through this data to find the particular student. This would be very time consuming and so a database system is typically equipped with a database management system (DBMS) that among other features also enables the user to search (or query) the database for a particular student record. Figure 1.1 shows that processing of data is done by querying the database and also that some other built-in tools are provided by the database management system.

Therefore, it is seen that in order to convert data into useful information a set of software tools are needed. The information that is processed will be used to produce reports and to make business decisions. One major aspect of electronic databases is that analysts using software tools that the DBMS supports can program them. In this way very sophisticated applications can be developed to include solutions that incorporate artificial intelligence (AI) techniques. This particular aspect can be extended so that it produces self-learning systems, which can optimise performance by making informed decisions about the behaviour of data. Having mentioned this it is fair to say that in this text we will not concern ourselves with artificial intelligence or knowledge based systems (KBS). This can be an aim for a future text for you to study and for me to produce.

1.2. Database Management Systems (DBMS)

The essential tools required to access the data are provided by the DBMS. [1,2,3] That is to say that when you purchase a licence to use a database such as for example, Microsoft Access you will also have the tools that help you to use the database efficiently. More details about using these tools are covered in Chapter 3 of this text.

Thus a DBMS is a collection of programs provided by the vendor, which enable the data to be accessed, filtered and generally processed efficiently, in order to yield useful information for the user. Figure 1.2 shows the basic components of a typical database management system.

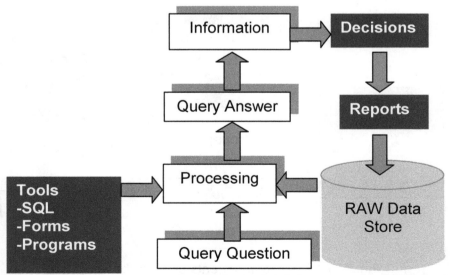

Figure 1.2 basic components of a typical database management system.

To the right of Figure 1.2 is the data store from where the raw data is available for processing. Typical processing example could be that the user submits a query and the DBMS provides the results to the query, which can be arranges as a report. For example, in a student record system the query could include a search for all the students in the final year of their degree who have an average mark of 70% or greater. This query will be processed and the results would produce a list of students that satisfy the criteria specified in the query. These results can be used to help with any decisions to be made. In this example the decision could be to award these students a first class honours degree, or perhaps to award a prize to the best performing student overall. Additionally a report can be generated that describes the details of these students and the degrees awarded to them.

Therefore in principle, user will generate a question (query) and the DBMS will search the dB to find the answer, which will be returned to the user. Typically a DBMS will include additional tools to provide graphical user interfaces and report generation programs to facilitate the delivery of information to the user. It will also provide tools to create, edit, process, and modify data and also to program the database. For example, SQL is a standard language used for accessing relational databases. Different relational databases such as Oracle, MySQL, MS Access etc, all have different procedural extensions to SQL. Procedural Language (PL) extensions to Structured Query Language SQL (PL/SQL) is Oracle's programming language, which provides procedural extensions in all Oracle environments. Visual Basic for applications is used to programme MS Access and PHP and Perl scripts can program MySQL.

All modern databases come with a DBMS and the analyst needs to learn how to use the tools within in order to work with the database. In essence DBMS tools are all designed to be user friendly, but in order to be able to deal with complex data, the user must learn the full set of features supported by the DBMS. There are occasions when the basic features of a DBMS are no longer able to cope with the needs of the user. In this case analyst programmers can be engaged to write programs to access the database and process the information in the desired fashion.

One of the most common languages for interrogating a database is the Structured Query Language (SQL) (pronounced sequel) and this language is supported in part by most DBMS systems. [5] However, each DBMS will have a few its own SQL commands, which are not part of the American National Standards Institute (ANSI). [6] Typically an SQL statement is an expression that defines a Structured Query Language (SQL) command, such as SELECT, UPDATE, or DELETE, and can include statements such as WHERE and ORDER BY. For example consider the SELECT command used to identify students in a database. The SQL statements could use the SELECT command as follows,

```
Example 1.
SELECT     Course_Number
FROM       StudentRecords
WHERE      student_name = 'Mickey Mouse';

Example 2.
SELECT     student_number
FROM       StudentRecords
WHERE      BEngCourse = '2388' AND average_mark
?70;
```

Looking at the code provided it is seen that the example 1 statements use the SELECT command to retrieve the course number FROM the student records database WHERE the student name is Mickey Mouse. So the actual statements are very similar to natural language queries.

The second example uses the SELECT statement with two conditions to retrieve from the database. This retrieves the student number of those students that are in course number 2388 and their average mark is greater or equal to 70%. Both statements are only accessing information stored in the StudentRecords database tables and returning to the user the results that satisfy the statements of the query. These simple examples indicate that SQL is a very useful tool for interrogating a database and that learning to use SQL is very much like learning a programming language. More details about using SQL with Microsoft Access will be covered in Chapter 3.

1.3. Types of databases

Electronic data storage is common to all computerised database systems. The types of databases that can be identified are driven to a large extent by the application. For example, if you are a university lecturer and you need to record attendance of students during laboratory sessions then you may well be a single user of this database and you would update the records after every lab session. You may be required to identify if a student has attended regularly and once again you would be the only user that needs to have access to this information. This type of database could therefore be considered to be a single user database. On the other hand, if the university regulations stated that a record of student attendance during all laboratory sessions must be available to the administration department, then each lecturer would have to maintain their attendance lists in a centralised database. In this case the database would be of a multiple user type (multi-user) and also it would be centralised. There are many more examples [1,2,3] but in general databases can be classified by User, Location or Type. These are briefly explained next.

Classification by user

This classification is made in regard to how many users the database is designed to support and this can be either a single user or multiple users.

Single user databases. This type of database is commonly encountered in desktop computers where only one user at a time can access, modify and generally use the database. Other users have to wait for this user to finish before they can access the database. A diagram of a single user database is shown in Figure 1.3. Here a single arrow shows that only one user at a time can be connected to the database. Therefore, this type of database does not support simultaneous access by multiple users.

It is worth pointing out that Microsoft Access was initially designed as a single user database. However with the broad use of Microsoft Windows operating system many companies that use Microsoft networks also try to use Microsoft Access in a multi-user configuration. Since Access was not designed to handle this kind of activity, there were problems. Two of the most common problems are given next. [7]

Data Corruption. This can happen when multiple users modify data at the same time and the database has not been designed to support this. The fact that users can change data simultaneously, when this is not supported by the DBMS, often causes data corruption.

Performance and Speed If the database is coded inefficiently then with multiple users this problem will become exaggerated and this in turn will cause the application to run slower. In other words the increased number of users multiplies the single user inefficiencies. In database applications this is commonly referred to as the bottleneck effect.

With the evolution of the Windows O/S in the networking arena Microsoft have solved many of these problems and now offer Microsoft Access multi-user solutions. Specifically, Microsoft Access provides tools and features for creating multi-user database solutions by using four different database architectures: file-server, client/server, replication, and Web-based data access pages. [8]

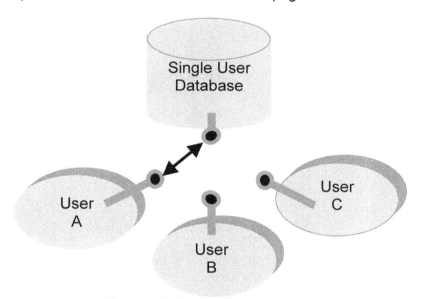

Figure 1.3 Single user databases

Multiple user databases

With this type of database, as shown in Figure 1.4, many users are able to access the database at the same time. There is only one database and each user can make independent changes in accordance with their user rights. If there are less than 50 users then this type of database is generally referred to as **Workgroup database**. Typically, for the number of users exceeding 50 the database is referred to as an **Enterprise database**. From Figure 1.4 it is seen that this type of database allows many users to connect to it simultaneously. It could be arranged that all users have full access rights to the database and can read, write and modify the content. In this case the DBMS ensures that the most up-to-date information is stored in the database. In order to facilitate multiple server databases across a network most configuration utilise the client-server model. In a general sense this means that the main application runs on the server, which supports many clients that are connected to it across a network. Typically, the server version of the software is much more elaborate than the client version of the application software and the two ensure that network communication is efficient and that the functionality of the client-server configuration is appropriate for the task in hand. Clients are referred to as thick or thin clients depending on how elaborate the software on the client is. Thin clients are cheaper and easier to configure, but they tend to have fewer processing features than thick clients and as a result they need more network bandwidth to communicate with the server where the main processing is done. On the other hand, thick clients can do much more processing without consulting the server and therefore consume less bandwidth, but they are more complicated to configure and more costly. Therefore the choice is very much governed by the application and the communication environment. In the business community multi-user databases are much more common than single user databases and therefore MS Access have provided solutions so that their databases can be used in a multi-user configuration.

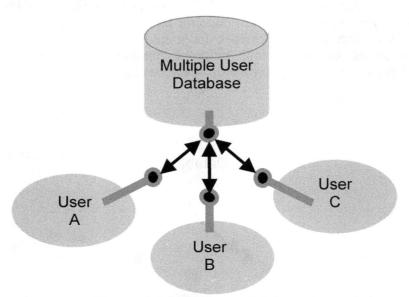

Figure 1.4 Multi-user databases

As mentioned earlier, Microsoft provides a number of solutions for the multi-user market. These are mentioned briefly next.

File-server: This is a straightforward network share solution where an Access database is configured as a network share so that multiple users can use it simultaneously. Here the database is in one location and it supports multi-user access through a network share, the DBMS includes tools to control the problems of data corruption. Note that this is different to the client-server model, because there is no difference between the shared version on the file server, and the version that is run by a computer using the share. That is to say, MS Access does not have separate server and client side software versions.

Client/server: In order to run in a client-server environment MS access must be configured to run as a client to a remote database server. For example an SQL Server could be used to share data between multiple users. Copies of the Access client application are then distributed to all users so that they can access the server database from their own computer.

Database replication: Microsoft networking supports replication though its directory services. Therefore it is possible to configure database replication so that an Access database can be shared among multiple users. Database replication is the process of sharing the changes between copies of an Access database in different locations without having to redistribute copies of the entire database. This involves producing one or more copies, called replicas, of a single original database, called the Design Master. Together, the Design Master and its replicas are called a replica set. By performing a process called synchronisation, changes to objects and data are distributed to all members of the replica set. Changes to the design of objects can only be made in the Design Master, but changes to data can be made from any member of the replica set.

Web-based database solutions: These are the extension to the multi-user solutions given above, except that they use Web pages as the front-end client application which are connected to a shared Access or SQL Server database.

Classification by location

By location, multi-user databases are classified as centralised or distributed depending on where the database resides. If is stored in a single location then it is centralised. On the other hand if the database is stored on a number of network nodes then it is said to be distributed.

Centralised database

In a centralised database system there is only one database, which is shared between users. This means that all modification that are made by users, are done to the master database and there are no working copies of this database. Figure 1.5 shows this type of arrangement where any number of users can access a single database that is stored in a particular location. This type of database tends to be common with workgroup databases discussed earlier. The main advantage of this is that all the updates are done on the centralised database and therefore it is up to date. It is also easier to maintain and more economical than distributed databases. This principle is used in Microsoft database solution as a network share discussed earlier.

Perhaps the main disadvantage of this type of database is that a failure of the network machine running the master database will prevent all users from using the database until the machine is back on-line. Another disadvantage is bandwidth restriction because all users have to communicate with the central database across the network. To overcome these disadvantages larger database applications tend to be of a distributed type. To provide a degree of security in the centralised configuration, regular backups need to be performed to prevent loss of data.

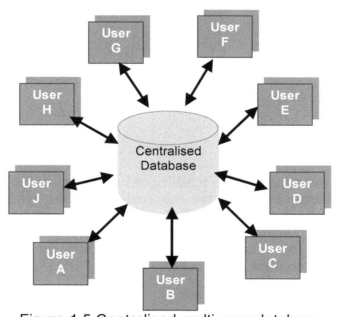

Figure 1.5 Centralised multi-user database

Distributed databases

A distributed database is commonly found in networks where it is configured as a single logical database, but parts of the database are located at different locations on the network. Although it is distributed across a number of servers on the network, the database behaves as a single entity. All the changes made to the database are replicated across all the servers that contain the parts of the database. Database replication can be used on many database management systems, usually with a master/slave relationship between the original and the copies. In this configuration, the master logs the updates, which are transmitted across the network to the slaves. Arguably, the main advantage of this arrangement is fault tolerance. This is to say that, if one of the servers is down, others can take over the workload. A major concern however is data integrity, because with parts of the database residing in different location, we must insure that there are no data conflicting data. In distributed databases data integrity is maintained by the use of replication. This is done to ensure that the same data are stored on multiple storage devices. Figure 1.6 shows a typical arrangement of a distributed database. Here the separate locations are seen to contain parts of the database and multiple users can access each of these. Users are in general free to read, write and modify the data in the same way that a multi-user database allows this. But unlike the multi-user solution, distributed databases contain replicas or duplicates across the network and this helps with fault tolerance.

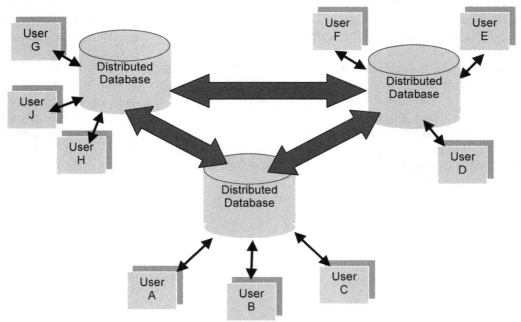

Figure 1.6 Distributed database

There are two ways to configure a distributed database; one is by replication and the other by duplicating the database. Replication involves synchronisation of the database across the network and this increases network traffic. Duplication on the other hand stores an identical copy of the database on another server. This can be useful when data is not changing too frequently, and therefore duplicating the changes is not frequently done. [9]

Classification by type

In many applications it is necessary to configure a database solution in accordance with the type of data that is stored. Thus, two major types are identified, a transactional database that changes frequently and records transactions, and a data warehouse, which contains data that are not changing frequently. For example, the British library has embarked on a project whose aim is to select and to digitise complete runs of UK newspaper titles that are published between 1800 and 1900. In this project it is proposed to select a mixture of UK national, regional and local newspaper titles, which reflect the social and political developments of the times in

8

which they were published. [10] Since this digitised data is in electronic form and once produced is not going to change frequently, a data warehouse solution is required. On the other hand, a database recording stock market trading needs to record data that are changing frequently and in this case a transactional database solution is required. Figure 1.7 shows a comparison of the types of information that is stored in transactional databases in comparison to data stored in a data warehouse. From Figure 1.7 it is seen that transactional databases are expected to hold data that changes frequently. For example, an on-line store will record the items purchased and therefore maintain a record of stock levels as well as the revenue generated from the sales. This will be changing throughout the day and so this type of data store is time critical.

On the other hand, a data warehouse is used to store data that does not change frequently. For example, a database that stores the inflation rate is maintained by the British government and available on-line. [11] This data could be used to analyse trends and perhaps make some political decisions to influence these trends. Therefore a data warehouse could be used to help governments to make strategic decisions because the data stored tends to be longer term. Consequently this data is considered to be NON-time-critical.

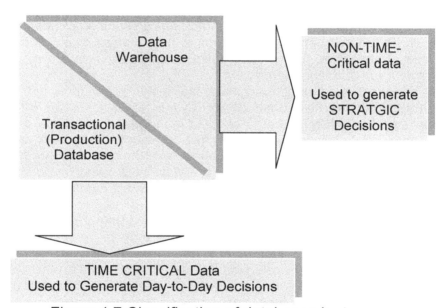

Figure 1.7 Classification of databases by type

1.4. Database design

Designing efficient databases is a major challenge for developers. An efficient database will enable users to enhance the performance of a business both in speed and quality of service to clients. For example, imagine a database designed to book air flights on-line. The client needs to have the confidence that when a flight has been booked and paid on-line, all the details are correctly entered into the database and can be retrieved quickly. At a very basic level a database contains the components shown in Figure 1.8. Here it is seen that tables contain records that are of a similar type. For example in a database for a town library you could have a table storing all the books that are available for loan. These records consist of collection of fields that are related. In the example used, the fields could be author, publisher, ISBN etc. Raw data is input into the fields and together these components constitute the database.

9

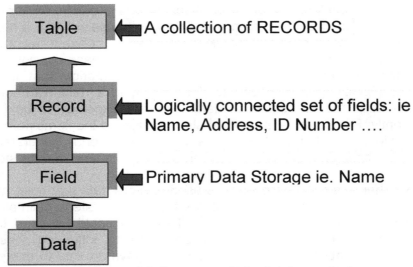

Figure 1.8 Components in database design

The design of a database is concerned with the way that these components are organised and this determines how efficient the design solution will be. In the example of a town library, the design has to determine how many tables will be used in the solution, and what records they will store. Poor design can result in repetition of data and also difficulty in updating records.

A very important consideration in database design is the tools that the database application supports. As mentioned earlier, every database comes with a database management system (DBMS) that is used to manage the database and offer users the tools to interrogate the database and make decisions. These tools are designed to help to design, run and maintain a database. Nevertheless, it has to be pointed out that the internal structure of the database solution will need to be designed for a particular application. This structure has to be planned carefully in order to avoid inefficiency in the operation of the database.

As an example, let us say that we need to design a database for a student record system. The first problem is to identify the entities that are relevant to the database solution and their attributes. These will in turn serve to help us define the tables, records and fields in our database solution. If we list the nouns for the system we can say that we have students, lecturers, courses, units etc. From these we can select the tables, which will hold the individual records corresponding to each occurrence of the entity. Assume that we select tables for lecturers, students and courses, then the lecturer table for example, will contain a record for each lecturer that is recorded. Next we use the adjectives to describe the nouns. In the lecturer record example, these could be, name, address, identification number, male, female, etc. From these attributes of the lecturer record we can draw up a list of fields that are required in order that we can keep track of every lecturer. By the same token, a student record in the student table could have attributes such as; Name, address, ID Number, Course, units etc, and these would be the fields in the student table.

Before we carry on describing database design we need to ask ourselves a few questions, for example:

- Do we know all the fields that we need to include so that our records and files contain all the necessary data?
- What fields will each of our records contain?
- Do we allow fields to duplicate in records? This will create data redundancy.
- What records are needed in tables?

These are the obvious questions that we can think of but there are many more. Note that these are only the initial design considerations and that the design will evolve as we proceed. For example, courses are nouns, but we can use it as a field in the student table to signify the course that the student is attending. In chapter 4 we will consider database design in more detail. But before we describe the details of database design let us consider some of the common problems that are caused by poor database design. Some of the general considerations in database design are considered next.

1.5.   Database design considerations

Data dependence and structural dependence

In a broad sense it could be said that main purpose for using a database is to enable the user to access information and to process this in order to make some decisions. Database designers need to organise the data into a structure that suits its application. Thus, there is a structural dependence associated with data in a database.

Structural dependence controls the mechanisms that are available for changing the structure of the database. An example of structural dependence is whether or not it is easy to add another field to a record in the table, and how will this impact on other tables. As a general rule database design must ensure that it is relatively easy to make the necessary modifications to the structure. The number of modification that can be expected will vary according to the application and this must be accounted for during the design process. For example, in a university students are expected to complete their course in a specific period of time, say three years. Therefore the student record system database must facilitate this frequency of data change. But we need to consider if this involves structural changes to the database. The immediate answer is, probably not. The students completing their course and the students registering on courses will not require structural differences in the database. The tables, and attributes will typically not require changes. However, if the UK government passes a law that requires each student to have a national insurance number field, then we need to introduce structural changes to the database.

It is also worth pointing out that in all database applications there is a relationship between individual data items. This is a consequence of needing a database in the first place. That is to say to store related data. Therefore during the design process, data dependence is concerned with data itself, rather than the structure. For example, data dependence will be concerned with how easy it is to change a field from say being a number to a text value. This could result because of a policy change to enhance security by adding letters to bank account numbers. Storing these modified account details would require a modification so that the account_number field is now a text field rather than a number. This change is likely impact on all data that has a direct relationship with this field. Good database design will ensure that the database can accommodate these changes without a major effort.

Data Redundancy

Data redundancy is perhaps the most common problem in database design. This occurs when the same data is stored in a number of locations. For example, a student's address could be kept in the finance table as well as in enrolment and exam results tables. Good database design will ensure that data are not duplicated by being stored in all three tables. This will save on storage space (memory) and also improve the speed of data access and processing.

Redundancy can also impact on data integrity, which refers to the consistency of data which is duplicated or in other words, data integrity is concerned with any conflicts in data values. For example, if our design requires us to maintain a student's e-mail address in a number of different locations, then failing to update an e-mail address for a student in all locations will result in data inconsistency.

Data anomalies

Modification, insertion and deletion anomalies all relate to data where a single record affects many other records. This is referred to as a one-to-many (1:M) relationship. We will consider cardinality of one-to-many, one-to-one and many to many later on but for now let us concentrate on data anomalies. For consider that there is one personal tutor for many students. So this is a one-to-many relationship and the database will keep a record indicating the personal tutor for each student, which means that many students will have the same personal tutor. If the tutor's telephone number changes then, because the relationship is one-to-many, the individual records of every student have to be updated with this new information. Failure to update will result in a data anomaly, which in this case is referred to as a modification anomaly.

Similarly we face problems with for example, introducing a new unit on a course. In this case the units are taken by many students (i.e. 1:M relationship) and so records for each student enrolled on the course will change. Therefore records for all students have to be updated accordingly, and failure to do this will result in an insertion anomaly or conversely a deletion anomaly.

1.6. Components of database systems

In order to ensure that the database has the correct structural and data dependence, modern database management systems (DBMS) will store data structures as well as relationships between this data. In this manner, by controlling access to data structures many of the anomalies mentioned earlier are removed. Figure 1.9 shows the main components of a database system. The actual database is shown in the right as data stores, and in the centre of the diagram the DBMS provides the control of data structure, relationships as well access control to these. Access control further implies security, which includes the system, processes, and procedures that protect a database from unintended activity. Security is usually enforced through access control, auditing, and encryption which are supported by the DBMS and the network operating system (O/S). [12]

Thus, a database system facilitates data management by regulating the collection, storage, protection and use of data. It follows that a database system will comprise of hardware and software components. The hardware part is fairly obvious but it is worth noting that besides the computer and peripheral hardware, computer networks hardware plays a significant role in modern database systems.

The software components include the operating system (O/S), DBMS and the additional tools including application and utility software. The operating system refers to the software that makes all the resources available to users. The resources usually include hardware such as printers, hard disks, network interface cards, multimedia equipment, but this can also include software, such as applications that need to be shared between users. Common operating systems include UNIX, Linux, Microsoft Windows, Mac and IBM z/OS.

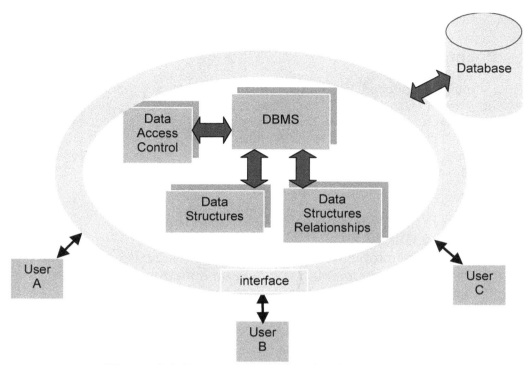

Figure 1.9 Components of a database system

Figure 1.10 Software – Hardware

Figure 1.10 shows the relationship between the software and the hardware in a database application. It is seen that the DBMS sits above the O/S and uses it to communicate with resources. It has its own software tools to help the users in their efforts to communicate with the database and obtain the required information. Common DMS include Microsoft Access, Oracle, IBM's DB2, Informix, UniVerse, and UniData. Application programs are written by analyst programmers and are used to access data in a database and produce information from this data that can aid users in decision-making. The programming is usually done in a high level language (HLL) such as C++, VB and programmers write interface routines to the DBMS so that they can access the data.

13

1.7. Chapter summary

This chapter introduced the basic features of electronic databases and briefly discussed their classification. This classification includes classification by user, location and type. The chapter further considers the general characteristics of centralised and distributed databases. We also briefly mention the main functions of the database management system. Some general ideas on database design are also considered although more detailed coverage is provided in Chapter 4.

Exercises

1.1. What are the main features of a database system?
1.2. What is a DBMS or rather what does it do?
1.3. What are the problems encountered in a multiple user database?
1.4. What are workgroup databases and an enterprise databases?
1.5. Explain the basic structure of a centralised database.
1.6. What is the main disadvantage of centralised databases?
1.7. What are the main disadvantages and disadvantages of distributed databases?
1.8. Distinguish between transactional database and a data warehouse.
1.9. How does DB Design relate to DBMS?
1.10. Why is DB design application dependent?
1.11. Why should we plan a data structure?
1.12. What are the components of a data structure?
1.13. What is the hardware part of a database system?
1.14. Give examples of the software components of a database system and explain how they relate to hardware?
1.15. In database design distinguish between structural dependence and data dependence.

CHAPTER 2 DATA MODELLING

2.1. Data models

Modelling is widely used in science and engineering in order to save time and money when developing a product. Models can give relatively accurate picture of how a system will behave before it is built. If the system model shows undesired behaviour then this can be corrected in design before the system is built. When the model is tested and found to conform to system specifications it can be built.

Data models use the modelling tools that are suitably defined to represent the flow of data through the system. The data structure is very important in database design because it can reduce the actual number of data components that are stored without diminishing the usefulness and availability of the data. A simplified diagram showing how modelling fits into the system development cycle is shown in Figure 2.1

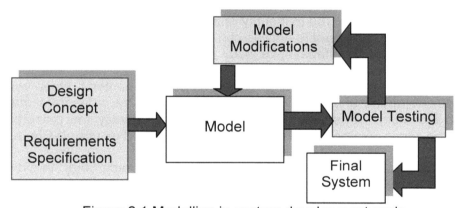

Figure 2.1 Modelling in system development cycle

Figure 2.1 shows that modelling is used to help the developers evaluate the solution to system development. Modelling saves time by allowing designers to evaluate and assess a system model before engaging in a full system development. It also true that at the outset, some of the requirements may not be clear, and the system model can help to clarify these. Figure 2.1 shows that when the model is built, it is tested and modified if necessary. This iterative approach allows the model to be refined until it behaves according to the desired specifications, at which point we can proceed with developing the final system.

All database design must start with a model in order to establish a data structure as well as relationships between data. A model provides a convenient and cost-effective option for design from concept to the final system through a number of iterations. At each iteration a model will be able to highlight any deficiencies in design, which can be corrected and the model tested again.

In database design there are a number of different models. The two most prevalent models to date are the relational model and the object-oriented model. We take a brief look at other models in order to gain an understanding of the need behind models. Since the introduction of electronic databases the way that data is stored and operated upon needed to be defined. This required a data model and over time a few of these were developed. These data models include,

- Hierarchical
- Network
- Relational

- Entity relationship
- Object Oriented
- Object-Relational

In this text we will cover only the essential features of these. For a more detailed explanation please see [13].

2.2. Database modelling basics

All databases contain entities, each of which has a set of attributes and these entities will typically have some kind of relationship with each other. Consequently it is useful to consider database modelling in terms of these three elements namely, **entities**, **attributes** and **relationships**.

Entity: This refers to the basic data description. An entity can be a physical object (i.e. person), a logical component (i.e. course), or simply a value (i.e. £100). If you find it difficult to identify an entity, simply think of nouns that exist in your system. These will often make it easier for you to identify entities. For example, if you are designing a database for a library, then some entities can be derived from the nouns that are used when describing a library database, i.e. book, user etc

Attributes: These are also called properties of an entity. These refer to properties that can be used to describe an entity. As mentioned in Chapter 1, when you need to identify the properties of an entity it often helps to list the adjectives that can be applied to the entity. These will serve the purpose to identify the properties of the entity. In the same example of a library attributes could be, title, ISBN, number of pages etc.

Relationships: These describe how entities relate to each other. In simple terms these can be thought of as links between entities. Thus, when an entity experiences a change, the link to another entity may cause a change in that entity as a result of their relationship. For example if a book is an entity then so is the user that loans it from the library. Therefore the two entities will have a relationship called 'loan' as a data component. If the book is withdrawn from the library, then it cannot be loaned out, so the relationship between the book and the user who wants to loan it determines the dependence between the two entities. (i.e. user and book) A database designer must take into account these relationships, and program them into the database in order that the database application functions efficiently and accurately. Another point worth mentioning is that relationships are classified in terms of how many objects (i.e. cardinality) are involved in the relationship. This was briefly mentioned in Chapter 1 where we identified three types of cardinality; namely;
- **One to Many (1:M)**: As in one lecturer to many students.
- **Many to One (M:1)**: As in many units to one course.
- **Many to Many (M:M):** As in many units to many students.

This classification is useful in database design to indicate the required data structure, which will also be influenced by data dependence.

Design constraints

All database design has to take into account the constraints on data. These constraints are sometimes called business rules and they control working practices of an organisation. For example, it may be a university policy that a class cannot run with fewer than five students. In the database design it is essential that the models reflect this rule. All models must allow the designer to describe these relationships and constraints on entities and their properties. Furthermore, the designer must be able to see where the models can generate problems, so that the design can be suitably modified.

2.3. Database model types

The Hierarchical Model

Perhaps the most intuitive database structure is the hierarchical model and for this reason, it was the first type of data model used in database design. The way that data is organised in this model is to define the root and then to introduce data levels below this root to segregate the data as shown in Figure 2.2. Thus the data structure resembles an inverted tree where the base of the tree is the highest level of hierarchy, and the branches below constitute the lower levels. In the library example, we can consider the root to be the entity book, below this other entities such as for example, fiction, educational etc. For each of these, another level of hierarchy can be introduced to further classify books by language, age group etc.

Figure 2.2 shows a single root that links to lower levels up to the lowest that is considered as useful for the database system. Thus it is seen that in this data structure the root is considered to be the parent of all objects below it and conversely, going down the structure each entity is the child to the one above it in the structure. In the hierarchical model it is clear that each child entity can only have one parent and that a parent entity can have many children entities. Whilst this is quite suitable for many database applications, the constraint that each child can only have one parent can restrict many database designs. Originally, hierarchical relationships were most commonly used in mainframe systems, but with the advent of increasingly complex relationship systems, they have now become too restrictive and are thus rarely used in modern databases. [14]

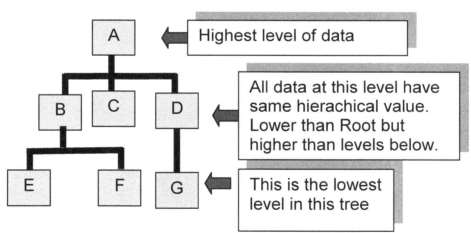

Figure 2.2. Hierarchical database structure

The development of database models has been evolutionary and continues to evolve, providing more advanced methods of representing the system during the design stage. The hierarchical model was the first used in database design and although it has been very useful, some modifications were necessary as database applications became more complex.

A significant limitation of hierarchical databases is that as a result of organising data on the basis of a parent/child relationship, each parent can have many children, but each child can only have one parent. Thus for example, if a student is enrolled on a course, then the course entity is parent to the student entity. But, what happens if we have a student who is enrolled on two courses? One full-time and the other part-time. The hierarchical structure could not deal with this problem efficiently.

Network Model

To improve performance the network model includes the ability of a child to have more than one parent. That is to say, in the library database example a user can loan more than one book and a copy of the same book can be loaned to many users. The data structure used in the network model can accommodate these relationships. The network database model expands the strict single-parent model of the hierarchical database in order to allow a record to have multiple parents. In this way the model can describe many to many relationships, and this enables a more realistic representation of the relationships between entities. It is worth noting that the terminology is somewhat different in the network model. Here the relationship between entities is called a set. Each set comprises of at least two records one the owner (parent) and the other the member (child). Thus, a set can show many members as well as many owners, and the single parent constraint is removed.

Although the network model was a significant improvement on the hierarchical model, there was a need for more flexibility in describing relationships between entities. This led to the development of the relational data model.

Relational database model

The relational database model is perhaps the most common type of model in current database applications and databases that subscribe to this model are called relational databases (RDBMS). Relational databases differ from hierarchical and network models, in the way that they organise data. In very simple terms a relational data model can be described as a collection of tables (with unique identifiers) to represent both the data and their relationships. Data are stored in rows and columns and the intersection of a particular row and column will point to a particular data value. This representation allows data to be a part of more than one table, and as a consequence tables can be linked together to represent relationships between entities. Thus, for example, a university student database could have an identifier for a course director, say CD_ID. This particular identifier can belong to a table storing student information and also in the table that is used to store the course director data, as shown in Figure 2.3.

table name	Student		
Student_ID	Student_Surname	Student_Course	CD_ID
201100	Lam	ECS-1-995	200100
201101	Bridge	ECS-1-103	200101
201102	Samuel	EMI-2-201	200102

table name	Course Director		
CD_ID	CD_Surname	CD_email	CD_Phone
201100	Bezanov	bez@lsbu.ac.uk	7532
201101	Bond	bon@lsbu.ac.uk	9090
201102	Al-Kharbi	alk@bbk.ac.uk	9091

Figure 2.3 Course director identifies is present in two tables

From Figure 2.3, the fact that the CD_ID exists in both tables constitutes a relationship between course_director and student tables. The DBMS enables the relationship to be implemented so that the actual data values for the CD_ID do not have to be entered into two separate tables. Therefore the possibility of data redundancy is reduced.

It should be clear at this point that relatively complex relationships could be described using the relational database model. To aid data analysis most relational databases support a query language called structured query language (SQL). It was mentioned in Chapter 1 that DBMS can be programmed to facilitate data processing, and that SQL is a common language used for this purpose.

The entity relationship diagrams (ERD)

In relational databases the ERD provide a graphical representation of entities and their relationships. In general, the ERD uses a rectangular box to hold the entity name and the diamond shape to hold the relationship. It also uses labels to indicate if the relationship is 1:1, 1:M or M:M. Straight lines between entities indicate connectivity. For example consider the following ERD representation shown in Figure 2.4. This shows that the personal tutor trains many students. Here the personal tutor and the student are entities and train is the relationship between them. This is shown as a diamond in the diagram, which is the convention, used in the Chen ERD model. Chen's notation for entity-relationship modelling uses rectangles to represent entities, and diamonds to represent relationships. [15]

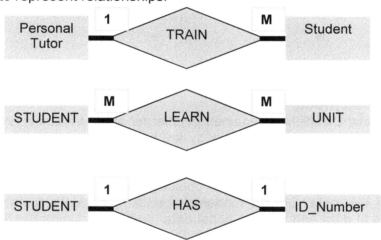

Figure 2.4 ERD representation

The second ERD in Figure 2.4 shows a many-to-many relationship between the student entity and the unit entity. This represents that many students can learn many units. The relationship between the entities student and unit is therefore learn. The last ERD depicts a one-to-one relationship between the entities student and ID_number; the relationship between them is has, because every student has only one ID_number. There are a large number of variants of ERD models and these can be found in literature. [1,2,3,13]

The symbols that are used to represent ER models tend to vary and perhaps the most common notation is the Crow's foot notation. This notation represents 1:1 and 1:M, M:M as symbols on the diagram rather than labels on the ERD. Additionally the relationship diamond is replaced with a simple label above the line. Thus, with Crow's foot notation the above diagram would be as shown in Figure 2.5.

The Crow's foot notation is very common and most database design applications on the market will allow the user to select the Crows Foot ERD model as a design tool. There are a large number of CASE tools that enable designers to develop relational database applications. For example, System Architect, Visio, PowerDesigner, ModelRight, Toad Data Modeler, DeZign for Databases, OmniGraffle, MySQL Workbench and Dia. [13]

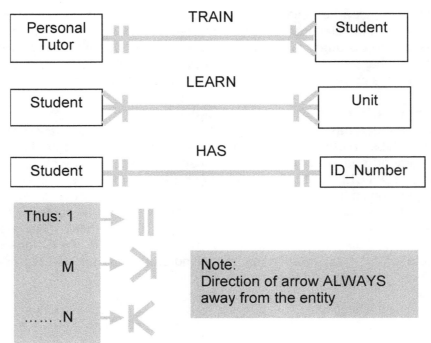

Figure 2.5 ERD representation using the Crow's Foot model

Object oriented model

The relational DBMS has remained popular for some time now however the most recent development in DMBS technology are based on the object-oriented database model. This type of model offers more flexibility than the hierarchical, network and relational models, but as a result of this it can be relatively complex to design. Under this model, data exists in the form of objects, which include both the data and the behaviour of this data. Certain modern information systems contain very complex combinations of data and the traditional data models (including the RDBMS) are not able to adequately model this complex data. For example, consider a hypothetical example of a database used to store current and previous values of commodities on the stock market. This information is valuable to traders because it enables them to analyse trends and so determine the best course of action. The change in the values of commodities is governed by a very complicated set of relationships and it is also determined by global events. For example a large world bank declaring bankruptcy will have a major impact on the amount of trading that goes on and this will impact on the value of these commodities. In such a database system the relationships between entities are very complex, and it is therefore very difficult to implement accurate and efficient database solutions.

The object oriented approach to database design attempts to model data in a way that resembles the real world. We are all familiar with objects that are around us and the way that we treat these or use them (i.e. car, book, etc). In object oriented models the trend is to embody data and relationships into an object, which more closely represents the behaviour of real-world entities. The word semantic implies learning and, the Semantic Data Model (SDM) aims to model the data as well as internal data relationships into a single structure called an Object. For this reason the SDM is referred to as the Object Oriented Data Model (OODM). The basic components of OODM are:

An object is similar to an entity in ERD and using the nouns in database design usually identifies it. An important distinction between an object and an entity is that an object represents one individual occurrence of the entity. Where many objects need to be considered the concept of a CLASS is used. Thus, a CLASS is a collection of similar objects. An object will have attributes (or properties) and those objects that have common properties will belong to the same CLASS. For example, an object-oriented structure of a database that is used to represent a university student database is shown in Figure 2.6. The entity student is associated with a number of properties such as ID number, course, lecturers etc. But not all students share the same mode of study. So the concept of classifying student into groups that share attributes gives rise to the concept of CLASS. In this way all full time students will consist of objects which belong to a separate CLASS to the part time students, although they will all belong to the student CLASS. The properties that all students have will belong to the student CLASS and can be inherited by the SUB-CLASSES. The unique properties that distinguish full time students from part time are identified within their respective SUB-CLASSES.

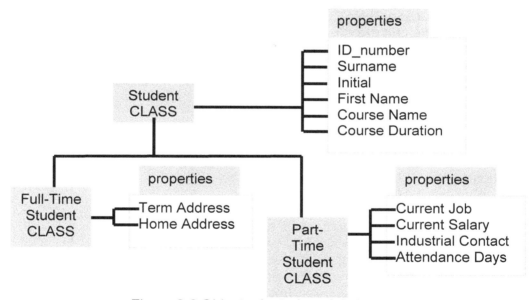

Figure 2.6 Object oriented model structure

Thus it is seen that in order to be able to differentiate between data that is similar, yet different in some essential features, the CLASS can be split up into SUB-CLASSES. The result is a CLASS hierarchy.

In a CLASS hierarchy the top-level CLASS lists the attributes shared by all objects in all classes and subclasses. Looking at the above diagram, the student CLASS will have properties such as ID_Number, surname, etc which are shared by all students whichever subclass they belong to. Each subclass will introduce a separate list of attributes that are prevalent in that CLASS only. Thus, during the design stage, the designer will choose how many separate classes are needed to implement the full data structure.

The object-oriented database model is generally considered to be more flexible and more manageable than its predecessors and it is also particularly good for modelling real-life systems. However the ability to model complex systems implies that this type of modelling embodies the complexity within its structure. This can

21

cause difficulties because the complexity is hidden from the user and tracing potential causes of errors in the database can be difficult. The OO data model is not necessarily aimed to replace the ER model; rather it is used in areas where it is the more appropriate solution to the problem.

Within this text we will focus primarily on the ER model and therefore we will consider this in more detail next.

2.4. Entity-Relationship (ER) modelling

As mentioned earlier data modelling provides a way to describe the nature and behaviour of data. By understanding the characteristic behaviour of data, analysts can obtain solutions to the problems inherent in creating, using, and managing the data. The database model must be well designed so that it represents the data efficiently and accurately. It serves the purpose to provide a specification for the design of the database.

In ER modelling the concept of business rules is used to describe the functional requirements of the database solution. Typically a discussion will take place between the database developer and the client, where an initial specification will be formulated. A useful approach to defining the requirements is to identify the business rules. These are the constraints that the developer must build into the design so that the business can benefit from the solution. Typically business rules will consist of statements, which describe the way that the operation runs within the organisation. Business rules can help the developer to identify define the following modelling components,

- Entities.
- Relationships.
- Attributes.
- Cardinalities.
- Constraints.

Some examples of business rules are as follows,

- A university has many departments.
- Each department belongs to a single faculty.
- Each course belongs to a single department.
- Each unit belongs to a single department.
- Each student has a unique ID number.
- Each student can be registered on more than one course.
- Each user registered in a library can loan many books.
- Each book has a unique ID Number.
- Each user must return the loaned book by a specified date.

In ER modelling the general approach is to use the business rules in order to identify entities and relationships between them (if any). Thus for example, from the above lists entities can be identified such as, university, faculty, department, course, unit etc. BY considering the business rules we can identify relationships. For example, the relationship between entities Course and Department is a many to one relationship, because there are many courses, and each of these belongs to a single department. The reverse is also true in that the department has a 1:M relationship with courses. In fact there is always a two-way relationship between any two related entities. In general relationships that are many-to-many are split up in ERD modelling so that they constitute two 1:M relationships. Such that M:M becomes M:1 + 1:M. This makes it easier to model and implement the database solution.

Example

Perhaps the best way to describe ER models is to provide a few examples. Consider that you have to develop an ER model for a local library; you could describe the following two business rules.

- Any book can be loaned more than once
- Any user can loan out more than one book.

This constitutes a M:M relationship between the entities user and book. As mentioned earlier, in ERM it is customary to break the M:M relationship into two relationships, namely M:1 and 1:M. This makes the design easier to follow. The way to do this is to introduce another entity (composite entity) between the M:M related entities, and this is called a composite entity. The resulting diagram is shown at the bottom of Figure 2.7.

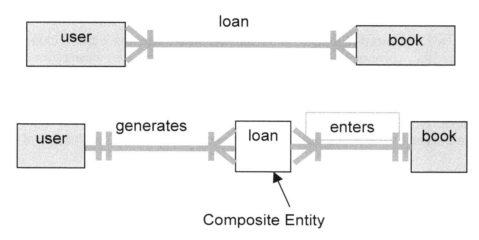

Figure 2.7 Composite entity used to reduce M:M models

The top diagram in Figure 2.7 shows that each user can generate many loans and that many loans can be entered for each book. In practical terms this means that the structure allows customers to loan out only one book per loan transaction. Therefore, it would be necessary to generate a separate loan transaction for each book loaned by a user. In other words, if a user wishes to loan out five books at a time, five separate entries need to be created. By introducing another entity called loan lines, the design could accommodate multiple book loans per transaction entered in the database. This is illustrated in Figure 2.8, where the entity 'loan line' is used to store the contents of the generated loans for users and books. Reading the diagram from left to right it is seen that every user can generate many loans each of which contains a single loan line and each of these describes a single book. But, because there are many loan lines, this allows a user to loan out more than one book, with each loan line representing a particular book loan. The solution is more efficient because we do not have to repeatedly enter the record for the same user for every book that they loan out. Instead we simply enter a new loan line for the user.

It has to be said at this point that the designer determines the number of entities and the relationships between them. Typically this will evolve through design and ER diagrams can be used to model the data structure and consider how successful it is in reflecting the business rules. Modifications to ERD models facilitate the evolutionary nature of the design with the aims to provide an efficient database solution.

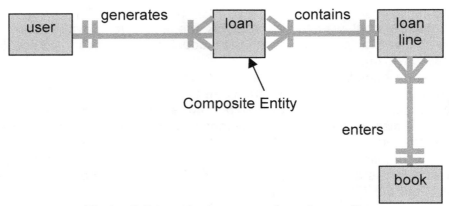

Figure 2.8 Introducing a new loan line entity

Thus a completed ER diagram can be seen as the actual blueprint of the database. Its composition must reflect accurately the operations within an organisation, in order to meet their data requirements. It helps to determine if the included entities, their attributes and relationships are appropriate and sufficient. The completed ER diagram also lets the designer communicate more precisely with clients and those who commissioned the database design. Finally, the completed ER diagram serves as the implementation guide to those who create the actual database.

Example

Assume that MIG Consulting Ltd has contracted you to create a conceptual model for a database solution to reflect the requirements for its training program. The client brief is as follows.

MIG Consulting Ltd delivers 4 separate courses to students for a fixed fee per student.
- There are 5 lecturers that deliver IT training and every one of these is trained to deliver a particular course.
- There is a maximum capacity in the classrooms of 12 students per class.
- If there are less than 6 students, the class is not economical and will be cancelled and the students refunded. It is, therefore, possible for a course not to generate any classes.
- One lecturer teaches each class, but every lecturer may teach up to two classes per day.

Given this information, you are required to define all the entities and relationships.

Table 2.1 provides the starting point for Entity Relationship (ER) Modelling of the problem. The table can be modified to reflect the business rules. Some of the points that need to be considered are listed below.

Table 2.1 The Components of the MIG ERD

Entity	Relationship	Cardinality	Entity
Lecturer	teaches	1:M	Class
Course	generates	1:M	Class
Class	is listed in	1:M	Enrol
Student	is written in	1:M	Enrol

Entity Relationship (ER) modelling example

For the above client brief, describe the relationship between lecturer and class in terms of connectivity, cardinality, and existence-dependence.

- A student can take more than one class, and each class contains many students (more than 6 and less than 12), so there is a M:M relationship between STUDENT and CLASS. Therefore, a composite entity (ENROL) is used as the bridge between STUDENT and CLASS.
- Only one lecturer teaches a CLASS, but a lecturer can teach up to two classes per day. Therefore, there is a 1:M relationship between LECTURER and CLASS.
- A COURSE may generate more than one CLASS, while each CLASS is based on one COURSE, so there is a 1:M relationship between COURSE and CLASS.

These relationships are all reflected in the ER diagram shown in Figure 2.9.

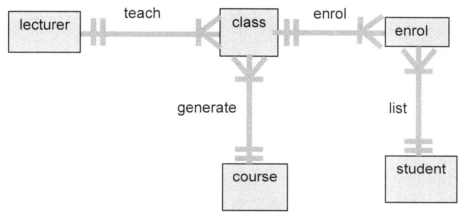

Figure 2.9 ER diagram solution

From Figure 2.9 it can be seen that each lecturer can teach many classes. Many classes make up one course. Many students can enrol onto a many classes, and this is represented though a composite entity. The ENROL entity reduces the M:M relationship between student and class into two separate 1:M relationships. This enables the data structure to record when students enrol on a selection of classes.

The above is only an example but it serves to show the principle of database design based on ER diagrams, and it should be sufficient as a starting point for modelling database design work.

2.5. Chapter summary

This chapter looked at modelling in database work. It introduced the various model types and offered a brief description for each of these. The entity relationship model is the most common at present and therefore this was considered in more detail. Chen and Crow's foot notation were presented as the commonly user notations in ERD modelling. Some examples of modelling using the Crow's foot notation were covered.

Exercises
2.1. Why is modelling needed in database work?
2.2. List and briefly explain the 5 different data models that are used in database work.

2.3. What are entity and attributes, and how can we identify them in database design?

2.4. Explain the significance of relationship between entities in dB work. A:

2.5. What type of relationships is supported in database design?

2.6. What are design constraints? Give some examples of these?

2.7. Use the crowfoot entity relationship model to describe the following relationships: (state any assumptions)

    i) Lecturer and his students

    ii) Student and his assignments

    iii) Car and road tax disk

    iv) Head, department, teacher, students

CHAPTER 3 MICROSOFT ACCESS

3.1 Introduction

As mentioned in Chapter 1, database is a software program that stores information, which relates to a particular activity or purpose. A database management system (DBMS) includes tools to help organise and maintain the data. Microsoft Access database provides a comprehensive set of tools to enable you to design, implement and maintain a database solution. Like everything else, you need to learn how to use these software tools before you can produce effective database solutions. Next, we will consider some aspects of these tools in relation to Microsoft Access.

3.2 Working with Microsoft Access database

Microsoft Access is a relational database package that runs on the Microsoft Windows operating systems. It comes as a component of the Microsoft Office package and has a very useful Help menu that can be used to introduce the application to a novice user. To use help, you need to start Microsoft access and click on the Help tab on the menu bar. From here you can navigate to the beginners menu as shown in Figure 3.1.

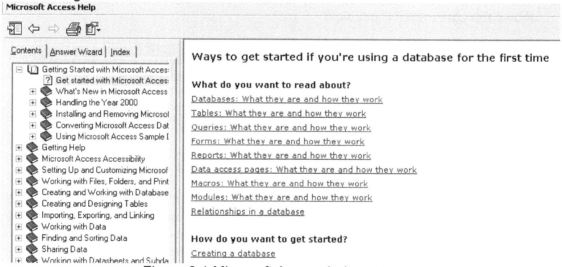

Figure 3.1 Microsoft Access help menu

You can click on the links and use the description provided to familiarise with the database. Some of these will be reproduced here for your convenience, but the full description can be found in the Microsoft Access help menu. [16]

Like all database application Microsoft Access supports features that enable you to implement a functional database application. These include the following,

- Tables to store data.
- Queries to interrogate the database and retrieve the data specific to the query.
- Forms that provide a graphical user interface to view and update data in tables.
- Reports to organise and print data in a specific layout.
- Data access pages to view, update, or analyse data from the Internet or an intranet.

There follows a brief selection of tips that have been compiled from the Microsoft Access 2003 Help system. [16]

3.3 Tables and relationships

All database applications use tables to store data. The designer of the database determines the number of tables that that are needed. Typically this means that the designer will create one table for each entity that is identified in the database. To put this into context consider that you have to develop a database for a library. In the simplest of forms the library will have registered users who will be able to take out books on loan. The database will also need to record which user took out which books. It would be possible to have a single table and to store all the information in that table. However this would be very inefficient and cumbersome for the following reasons.

For every user the database would need to record every book that they have taken out. So if a user named James Smith takes out a book called database fundamentals then the table can be used to record this information. If another user called Robert Taylor takes out another copy of the same book, then this is recorded in the table as a new record. If James Smith further decides to take another book out called Internet and Databases, then this constitutes another record in the table. So the table contains information, which is repeated, in other words it has redundant information. Figure 3.2 shows the contents of the table.

	ID	User Name	Book Title
	1	James Smith	Database Fundamentals
	2	Robert Taylor	Database Fundamentals
	3	James Smith	Internet and Databases
▶	(AutoNumber)		

UsersAndBooks : Table

Figure 3.2 contents of the table used in the example

From Figure 3.2 it is seen that the database user has to type in the name of the user twice and the name of the book twice. This is considered inefficient because you are typing the same information twice and also you are storing it twice, using computer memory unnecessarily. To make the database more efficient we can design two tables. One to store users and the other to store books. We then set up a relationship between these tables so that when a user takes a book out, the relationship between the tables is used to describe the action of loaning a book out. So the relationship between the table called users and the table called books is a many to many relationship called loan. An entity relationship diagram as shown in Figure 3.3 can describe this relation. Figure 3.3 also illustrates the graphical interface that MS Access provides for creating relationships.

This type of relationship allows queries to be set up to search users in order to find out what books they loaned out, or conversely to search which users took out a copy of a particular book. This is only a very simple example, but it serves to show how the choice of entities can influence the efficiency of the database. Therefore in order to bring the data from multiple tables together in a query it is necessary to define relationships between the tables.

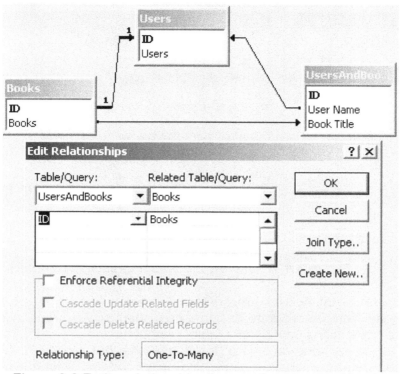

Figure 3.3 Entity relationship diagram for users and books

A unique ID is used for each table in Figure 3.3 so that it is possible to uniquely identify each record. This identifier is called the Primary Key and each table must have one. In order to define a relationship with another table this key is used as a Foreign Key in the related table. Therefore, by adding one table's unique ID field to another table and defining a relationship, Microsoft Access can match related records from both tables so that you can bring them together in a query. In Figure 3.3 it is seen that the relationship between the entities UsersandBooks and Books is a 1:M relationship. The ID field in UsersandBooks can loan out many books in the Books table. This is a trivial example but it serves to show how relationships can be created. If you wanted to find out from the database, which books were loaned to which users, then you would have to generate a query, in order to ask the database for the answers that matches the query.

Queries

Queries are used to find the desired data. The basic principle is to ask the database to retrieve the data that satisfies the conditions specified in the query. In the simple example of a library a query could be constructed to find all the users who loaned the book entitled Database Fundamentals. An example of such a query is given in Figure 3.4. There are three views shown in Figure 3.4. The leftmost view is the query as seen in design view, where the query checks the show box for all the books in the books table. Top right is the datasheet view, that describes the results and here it is seen that there are two books in the books table. Bottom right is the equivalent SQL command to specify the query. This can be seen by selecting the view SQL button form the MS Access menu bar. This is a very simple example, and this was intended in order to demonstrate the ways that queries are used in MS Access.

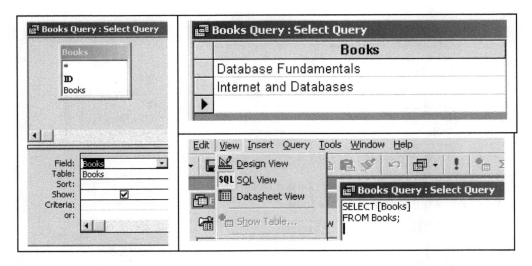

Figure 3.4. A simple query and the result of running it.

Forms

Forms in Microsoft Access are graphical object that helps you to work with the data. They offer you the option to design a graphical user interface to view, enter and perform other operations on data in a table, without having to edit the table to do this.

A table displays many records at the same time, but you might have to scroll to see all of the data in a single record. Also, when viewing a table, you can't update data from more than one table at the same time.

A form focuses on one record at a time, and it can display fields from more than one table. It can also display pictures and other objects.

A form can also contain a button that prints, opens other objects, or otherwise automates tasks.

Reports

The processing of data is usually done in order to provide users with useful information about the status of entities. For this reason, reports are used to arrange the results into templates that are easy to read. For example, you might print one report that groups students according to whether they paid their fees or not and another report to show how well the students performed in their examinations.

Some examples of creating forms and reports are given in the exercises at the end of this chapter.

Tables

Tables organise data into columns (called fields) and rows (called records). For example, each field in a Student table contains the same type of information for every student, such as the student_name, ID_number. Each record in that table contains all the information about one student. Figure 3.5 illustrates a typical field in a student table. This table was created in Design View within MS Access. This view enables you to create records by identifying the fields that are appropriate, and describing their data type. (i.e. text, number etc). The fields shown in Figure 3.5 are arbitrary and they have been created in this way. Once again we have to say that each table must have a primary key. So far in Figure 3.5 we have not identified it, and when the table is closed a warning will be displayed from the Access DBMS, that the table does not have a defined primary key. Tables without primary keys cannot function correctly with other tables because a unique identifier for a record in the table has not been specified.

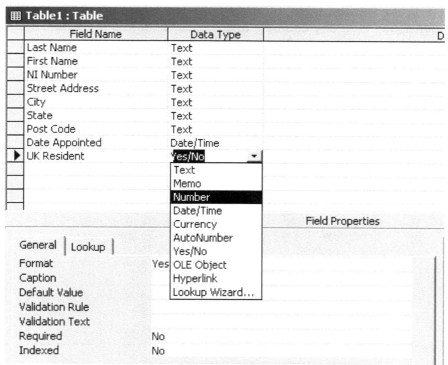

Figure 3.5 Fields used to describe students in a table

Table Design view

Microsoft Access offers you the option to create a database in Design View. In table Design View, you can create an entire table from scratch, or add, delete, or you can customise the fields in an existing table. For example you could select to create a new table, and create the fields as shown in Figure 3.5. Setting a field's data type defines what kind of values you can enter in a field. For example, if you want a field to store numerical values such as student ID_number, then you will need to set its data type to number. If you want to track additional data in a table, such as the student address, phone number, etc., you would use the design view to add more fields. Some basic operations with data in design view are covered in the exercises at the end of this chapter.

Primary key and foreign key

As mentioned earlier every table must have a unique identifier that is called a primary key, to identify each record in your table. A table's primary key can also be used to refer to related records in other tables.

A field, which is common to two or more tables, can be used to describe a relationship between these tables. In one table, the field is a primary key that you set in table Design view. That same field also exists in the related table as a foreign key. For example, in the Course table, you enter a Course_number, name, semester, and so on, for each course that you are tracking in the database, Course_number is the primary key that you set in table design view for this table.

In the lecturer table, the primary key used in the ni_number of the lecturer. Now, the lecturer table does not have a field to show the course that the lecturer teaches, but the course table does have a field called lecturer_id. In order to relate the two tables you could include the ni_number as foreign key in the courses table, so that you can identify the course that a lecturer is teaching. Figure 3.6 shows how this relationship is displayed in Access. The lecturer_id in the course table is related to the ni_number in the lecturer table, by a many-to-one relationship. This means that each lecturer can teach on many courses, and the identifier in the courses table that keeps track of this is the lecturer_id. This is not a primary key because it can occur in more than one record, since the same lecturer can teach on many courses.

At the bottom of Figure 3.6 it is seen that the windows for editing relationships also has the option to enforce referential integrity. This will be discussed later, but for now it is fair to say that this ensures data consistency between tables.

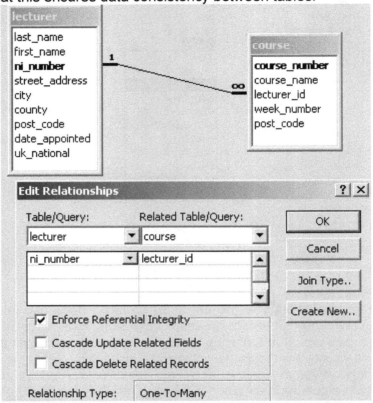

Figure 3.6. Relationships in Access using primary and foreign keys

Types of queries

Figure 3.7 MS Access query tools

There are a number of ways that a database can be queried and in MS Access this is done by different types of queries. Some of these are briefly described next, but a more detailed explanation is provided by MS Access help. [16]

MS Access provides the tools to create and describe queries under the menu bar as shown in Figure 3.7. There are a variety of queries that you can describe and these will be discussed next.

Select queries

Perhaps the most common type of query is the select query. This is used to retrieve data from one or more tables and to display the results in a datasheet. It is also possible to define a select query in such a way as to group records and perform some basic calculations such as sum, average, and other types of totals. The query described in Figure 3.4 earlier is an example of a simple select query.

Parameter queries

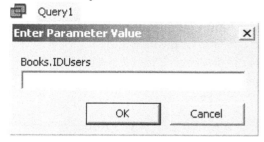

A parameter query is used for you input the required information through a dialogue box. You can design the query to prompt you for more than one piece of information; for example, you can design it to prompt you for two dates. AN example is shown to the left where the parameter query prompts the user to input a value for the Books.IDUsers field. This allows you to pick out different users each time you run the query by supplying different values for the parameter.

Crosstab queries

These queries are used to calculate and restructure data for easier analysis, and they display data in spreadsheet format. Crosstab queries calculate a sum, average, count, or other type of total for data that is grouped by two types of information one down the left side of the datasheet and another across the top. Figure 3.8 shows a comparison of select and a crosstab queries. [16]

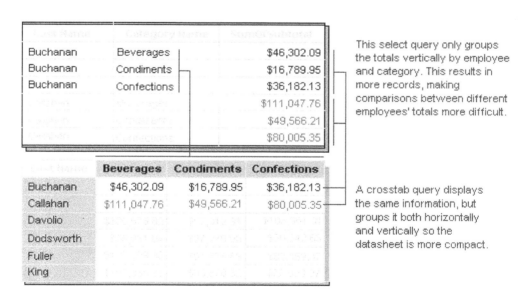

Figure 3.8 Select and crosstab queries in MS Access

Action queries

An action query makes changes or moves many records in just one operation. The following are the various types of action queries.

- **Delete Query**. This query deletes a group of records from one or more tables. For example, you could use a delete query to remove students that have withdrawn from a course. With delete queries, you always delete entire records, not just selected fields within records.

- **Update Query**. This query makes global changes to a group of records in one or more tables. For example, you can raise the fees by 10 percent for all the courses that you run. With an update query, you can modify data in existing tables.
- **Append Query**. This query adds a group of records from one or more tables to the end of one or more tables. For example, suppose that you transfer a group of students between two courses. You therefore need to include them in a database containing a table of information for their new course. To avoid typing all the information into the database, you could define an append query to find the new students and append these to the Courses table.
- **Make-Table Query**. As the name implies, this query creates a new table from all or part of the data in one or more tables. Make-table queries are helpful for creating a table to export to other Microsoft Access databases or to create a history table that contains old records.
- **SQL query.** You can use Structured Query Language (SQL) to query, update, and manage relational databases such as Access. When you create a query in Design view, Access constructs the equivalent SQL statements to represent this query. This was briefly illustrated in Figure 3.4 earlier. If you want, you can view or edit the SQL statement in SQL view. However, after you make changes to a query in SQL view, the query might not be displayed the way it was previously in Design view.

Examples of how to use these queries are covered in some detail in the help menu for Microsoft Access.

3.4 Macros

Macros are a set of actions that you can create to help you to automate common tasks. By using groups of macros, you can perform several tasks at once. These statements are written in a macro language that the application can interpret. In Microsoft office applications Visual Basic is used as the macro language. A macro is a set of one or more actions where each performs a particular operation, such as opening a form or printing a report. Macros can help you to automate common tasks. For example, you can run a macro that prints a report when a user clicks a command button.

When you create a macro, you enter the actions you want to carry out in this portion of the Macro window as shown in Figure 3.9.

When you create a macro, you enter the actions you want to carry out in this portion of the Macro window.

You can specify arguments for an action in this portion of the window. Arguments provide additional information on how to carry out the action, such as which object or data to use.

Print Invoice : Macro	
Action	
▶ OpenReport	Open the Invoice report
Action Arguments	
Report Name	Invoice
View	Print
Filter Name	
Where Condition	[OrderID]=[Forms]![Orders]

Figure 3.9. Example of using macros in Access [16]

You can specify arguments for an action in this portion of the window.

A macro can be one macro composed of a sequence of actions. Figure 3.10 shows a macro composed of a series of actions. Microsoft Access carries out these actions each time the macro runs.

Action	Comment
	Attached to the Add
Echo	Freeze screen while
OpenForm	Open the Product List
▶ MoveSize	Position the Product L

Review Products : Macro

Figure 3.10. Macro composed of a sequence of actions

Thus when you run this macro the three actions that it contains will be executed in sequence. Macros can also be grouped together and executed in the same manner. The name in the Macro Name column identifies each macro. When you run a macro in a macro group, Microsoft Access carries out the action in the action column and any actions that immediately follow with a blank Macro Name column. There are many other features that you can achieve with macros and examples can be found under the Microsoft Access help menu. [16]

3.5 Microsoft Visual Basic Editor

As mentioned earlier Visual Basic is the language that you can use to manipulate the files created in Microsoft Office applications. The Microsoft Visual Basic Editor (VBE) is the development environment in which you create and edit Visual Basic for Applications (VBA) code. You run Visual Basic code in Microsoft Access by running a Sub procedure or Function procedure. Procedures are stored in units called modules and they contain a series of statements and methods that perform an operation or calculate a value.

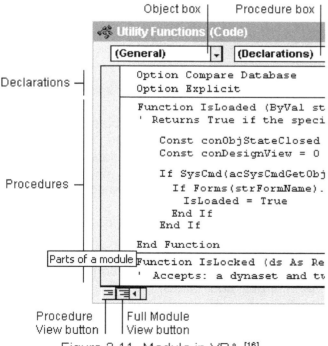

Figure 3.11. Module in VBA [16]

In VBA a module is essentially a collection of declarations, statements, and procedures stored together as one named unit. Figure 3.11 shows the structure of a typical module. At the beginning of the module are the declarations and this is followed by the procedures associated with the module.

VBA code can be used to automate functions that your database requires. It is a very powerful tool and I have only given it a brief mention here so that you are aware that it exists. For a more comprehensive treatment of using VBA you are advised to look up literature on the subject. [16,17]

35

3.6   Relationships

Relationships between tables indicate how the data in those tables is related. Typically you would design tables so that data is not repeated. But sometimes, tables require data that is stored in another table. To make this data available you need to define relationships between these tables. When you have done that, you can create queries, forms, and reports to display information from several tables at once.

A relationship between tables works by matching data in key fields. In most cases, these matching fields are the primary key from one table and a foreign key in the other table. For example, lecturers can be associated with contact hours that they are teaching by creating a relationship between the ni_number fields in both tables. This is shown in Figure 3.11. In this manner the primary key ni_number is used as a foreign key in the contact_hours table.

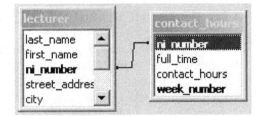

Figure 3.11. Creating a relationship between tables using foreign keys

From Figure 3.11 it is seen that ni_number appears in both tables. In lecturer table it is the primary key and in the contact _hours table it is a foreign key. The kind of relationship that Microsoft Access creates depends on how the related fields are defined:

- A one-to-many relationship is created if only one of the related fields is a primary key or has a unique index.
- A one-to-one relationship is created if both of the related fields are primary keys or have unique indexes.
- A many-to-many relationship is really two one-to-many relationships with a third table called the composite entity, whose primary key consists of two fields; namely the foreign keys from the two other tables.

3.7   Referential integrity

Referential integrity is a database concept that ensures that relationships between tables remain consistent. When one table has a foreign key to another table, the concept of referential integrity states that you may not add a record to the table that contains the foreign key unless there is a corresponding record in the linked table. Within MS access when you establish a relationship between tables you are given the option to select the enforce referential integrity checkbox. This was mentioned earlier with reference to Figure 3.6. You can set referential integrity when all of the following conditions are met:

- The matching field from the primary table is a primary key or has a unique index.
- The related fields have the same data type.
- Both tables belong to the same Microsoft Access database.

The following rules apply when you use referential integrity:

- You can't enter a value in the foreign key field of the related table that doesn't exist in the primary key of the primary table.
- You can't delete a record from a primary table if matching records exist in a related table.
- You can't change a primary key value in the primary table, if that record has related records

3.8   Chapter summary

This chapter introduced Microsoft Access database and provided an overview of how data is represented, in tables, records and fields. Features such as creating tables, using forms and reports and also querying the database were introduced. Examples of these are given at the end of the chapter under the exercises sections, and these follow from the topics covered in the main body of the chapter. We also briefly introduced macros and Visual Basic for Applications (VBA) as tools that enable us to automate the database solution. These were covered very briefly in order to provide an insight of what they can do for an application. A look at relationships between tables and how referential integrity can be maintained are also covered briefly.

Exercises

This laboratory activity is aimed at familiarising you with the Microsoft Access working environment. This will be achieved by guiding you through a set of exercises that will explore the features of Microsoft Access. While performing the exercises please ensure that you save your work so that you can refer to it as necessary.

Exercise 3.1.Open a database file

Detail
Log onto Windows
Turn on your PC Wait for Windows to Load Log onto Windows using the following credentials **Username:**<your username> **Password:** <your password>
Start Microsoft Access
To start ACCESS **Start** button and follow the menu to →Programs → Microsoft Access
Create a New database file
From the Access graphical user interface (GUI) menu-bar check the Blank Access database box and press OK to open a new database as shown below. 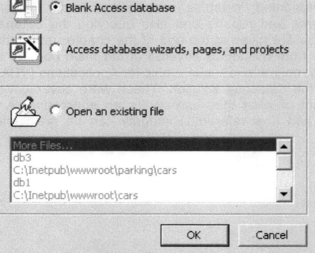 This opens a new database file with a default name **db1**. If you like you can change this as well as the path to the file.

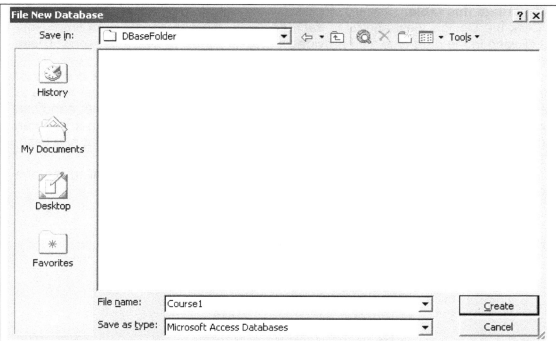

Change the name to **course1** by typing this into the File name window. Click the create button in the bottom right hand corner and you will get a Main Objects Menu (MOM) screen as shown below.

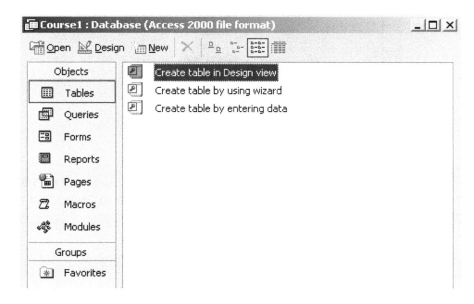

Here you have a choice of Objects on the left, each of which will have further options on the right pane. Thus the Tables object has a choice of create table in design, using a wizard or by entering data.

Creating Tables

Assume that your database will contain data about lecturers delivering a course.

To create a new table click New, Design View and give the table name Lecturer.

Assume that the fields the table contain information such as: Last name, First Name, NI Number, Street Address, City, County, Post Code, Date Hired and UK National.

To create this table:

Click the Design View and fill in each field with the appropriate data type. Note that clicking in the data-type filed provides a drop-down list of available types. These are self-explanatory.

I tend to write all my data in lower case letters and when the data consists of more than one word I join these with an underscore. This makes it easier for me to check for spelling and other typing errors in my database. You on the other hand can select a different labelling approach, but you must be consistent so that you can work more efficiently. Remember that data in tables is sensitive to spelling and case, so a spelling error will cause problems in the database.

When you have entered all the data you should have a table similar to the one given below.

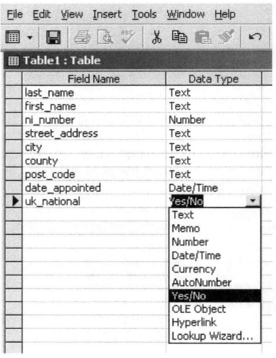

When you have finished choose File-Save and save the file under the name **lecturer**. You will note that when you try to save the file a message appears that the primary key has not been defined.

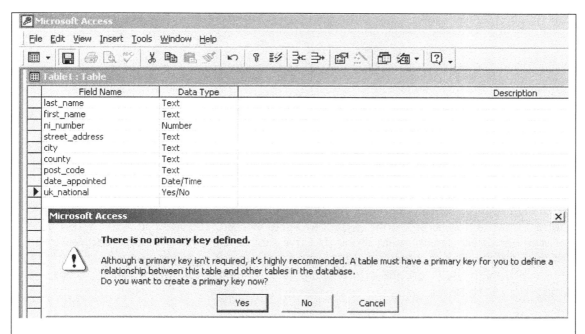

A **Primary Key** is a data field that uniquely identifies each record in the table. Thus it must be selected in such a way that no two or more records share the same value. ni_number is a good choice, so make this your primary key for the lecturer table.

Click Cancel to stop the automatic generation of primary key.

Click the NI Number prefix area to select it. Go to the menu and select the key icon ![key] to make this the primary key. Alternatively, right click the ni_number, and select primary key, as shown below.

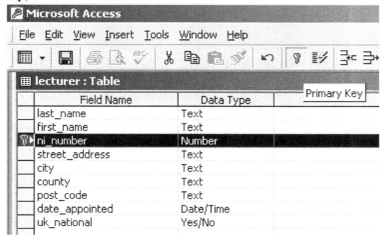

Be sure to save this table by naming it lecturer. Close this table after you have done this. You can see that you now have one table listed in your database.

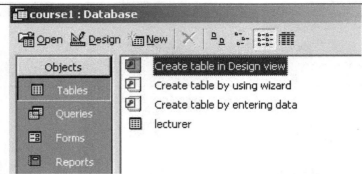

Assume that you want to monitor the workload of lecturers so you will create another table and call this contact_hours. This indicates the amount of time lecturers spend in contact with students. Typically lecturers are required to spend 18 hours per week in direct contact with students. The rest of the time they are required to do self-managed scholarly activity (SMA). (and this includes writing textbooks)

From design view, create a new table and fill in the following details. Save the table as contact_hours.

	Field Name	Data Type
🔑	ni_number	Number
	full_time	Yes/No
	contact_hours	Text
▶	week_number	Number

Note here that some employees are full time (40 hours every week), while some are part-time and their hours will vary. For this reason the full_time (Yes/No) field is used to describe whether the rate is for Full Time or not.

Once again make ni_number the primary key and save the table as contact_hours.

We could create more tables to show the courses that lecturers teach and other information, but in order to demonstrate the features of Access we will keep the number of tables to two. The principles can be extended to more tables if required.

Compound keys

From the contact_hours table note that the primary key is the ni_number. Also we have a record that describes the week number that a lecturer has worked. If a lecturer has worked more than one week, then their ni_number will be repeated. Therefore searching the database table by unique ni_number will not always produce a uniquely defined record.

This is because a lecturer may work a number of weeks (**week_number**), and therefore the lecturer's **ni_number** will be repeated. In this case we use what is called a **Compound Key** as the **primary key** in the contact_hours table. Which is to say that we combine two fields to uniquely identify a table record.

To make a compound key that contains the two fields, click in the first fields prefix area, pres Cntrl and select the other field to highlight it. Click on the key icon to select the primary (compound) key. Note that both the ni_number and the week_number fields show the primary key icon next to them. This means that they are part of a compound key. You can have more than two fields describe the compound key if this is required.

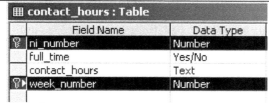

Save this table and close it.

At this pint the two tables have been created but there is no data. The field corresponding to the tables define will need to be supplied with actual data.

We will do this next.

Exercise 3.2. Inputting data

Add records to tables

In exercise 1 we created the tables that will hold data. We did this in design view and we selected the fields that our data will contain. We gave these fields their names and data types. Thus the data structure has been defined. The next step is to fill in the actual data into these tables. This is done in the datasheet view.

At the main objects menu (MOM) select Tables then lecturer. Then select Open. This opens the table in the datasheet view, which allows you to input the data. The data entry screen appears as follows.

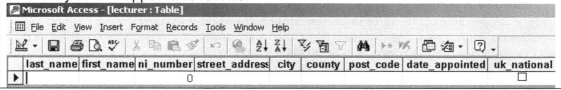

The table for data entry has all the fields that were created for the table in design view. To enter data you simply type in the information one field at a time. Each time that you write a value in a field, press Enter, and the cursor will move to the next cell.

After the last cell in a row, the cursor moves to the first cell in the next row and Access automatically saves the record, and you do not have to perform a file save operation at this stage.

Enter the data into the tutor table as shown below.

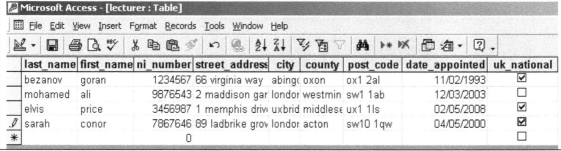

Enter Data into contact_hours Table

At the main objects menu, select contact_hours. Then select Open. In a similar fashion as before enter the data corresponding to the fields. Note that you have to make sure that the ni_numbers that you key in are the correct ones according to those used in the lecturer table.

⊞ contact_hours : Table			
ni_number	**full_time**	**contact_hours**	**week_number**
1234567	☑	18	1
3456987	☐	6	1
7867646	☑	14	1
9876543	☑	12	1
▶ 3456987	☐	6	2

Enter this data and when you have finished save changes and close the table.

You now have two tables with data and the next step is to process this data. We will look next at ways to query a database so that we can retrieve the desired information.

Exercise 3.3. Creating Queries

Create a Query

In exercises 1 and 2 we created the tables and entered the data that represents the contact hours for lecturers and the relevant information.

One of the main reasons for storing data in a database is so that you can retrieve it when necessary. The general term used for this action of retrieving data is to Query the database. A query is formulated using an SQL statement and the DBMS applies the criteria in the query to retrieve matching data.

There are a number of types of queries as discussed earlier in this chapter, but if a query simply selects or sorts data, the subset is called a dynaset.

Queries in Access are created from the main menu by selecting Queries. You can create a query in Design view or by Using wizard.

As the names imply, design view allows you to specify components of a query, and the wizard makes this process more user friendly.

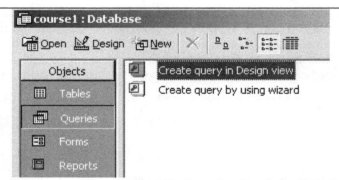

Note that by clicking on the queries button to the left, the two options are presented on the left. We will use the design view in order to create a query.

For now select Design view by double clicking it. This will give you the option of choosing one of the tables that you have already created. That is;

Select the lecturer table and click Add to begin adding a query. The Query design view window is displayed and you are presented with a list of fields that are available in the lecturer table. The dialogue box remains open so that you can add other tables if necessary. Click the Close button, the dialogue box shows the Select Query Window as shown below.

On the top you have a scroll box showing the fields that are available in the table, and the primary key (ni_number) is shown in bold.

At the bottom is the query window, which allows you to define the query. In Access this is called the Query By Example (QBE) grid. The query options that are provided to query the data shown in rows indicating the Field, Table, Sort, Criteria and Or.

To define a query you add the fields that you want to include in the query to the Field row of the QBE. You can include as many fields as you wish here, but there must be at least one, otherwise the query will not run.

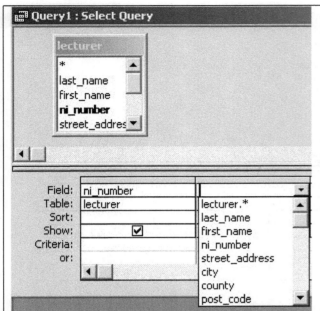

In the field list in the top half of the display select the NI Number field. (This also happens to be the primary key)

To use this field in a query, drag it down to the Field row of the QBE grid. Note that the Table name is automatically filled in, and a tick is selected in the show checkbox to indicate that the field will be used in a query. The arrow on the right of the field shows that you can select options for this field. Similarly, you can drag any other field that you want to use in the query.

To add another field, click the second column of the Field row in the QBE grid and select surname. To select another click on the third column and select city. This will define a query based on the ni_number, last_name and city of the lecturer. You can save the query under your desired title but the default is to save it Query1. Do not close it yet because you want to see the results of running the query.

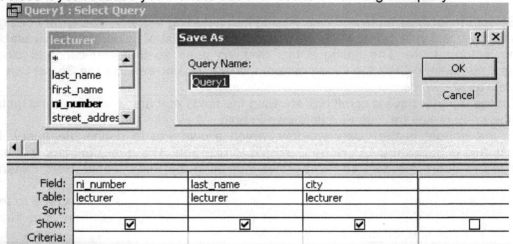

Click the View button on the toolbar and select datasheet view. This will display dynaset, which as you have specified, contains three fields, ni_number, last_name and city. Thus you are only looking at the dynaset and not at the complete table.

ni_number	last_name	city
1234567	bezanov	abingdon
3456987	elvis	uxbridge
7867646	sarah	london
9876543	mohamed	london

You can define additional criteria in your query by using the options in the QBE. Assume that you want to sort the data in ascending order and that you want to find all lecturers in London.

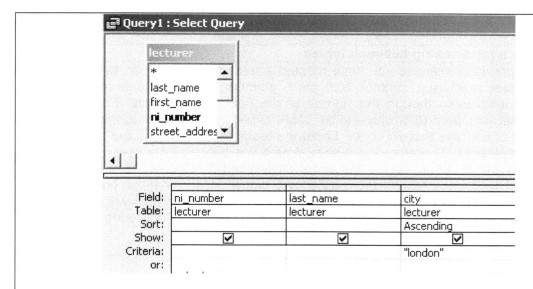

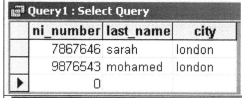

The datasheet view would display the dynaset of the results. That is all lecturers in London arranged in ascending order.

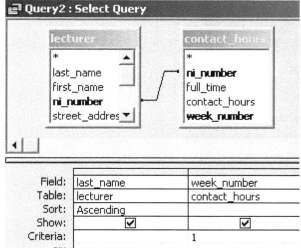

You can create more queries and also use different tables in the query. For example, you want to find out all the lecturers that have worked in week 1. You create another query called query two and you add both tables to the query.

Note that when you add more then one table, the primary keys of both tables are highlighted, and the relationship between them is shown with a line. In this case the ni_number is common to both tables and it is used to link the records.

As before to define the query you select the fields that you want to use, i.e. last_name from the lecturer table and week_number from the contact_hours table. You set the criteria for week number to 1.

In datasheet view the results will show the dynaset corresponding to the criteria specified in query 2.

There are many more features in Access that you can use with queries but here we are only introducing the fundamental concepts. These should be enough to get you started, and you can improve with practice.

Exercise 3.4. Creating relationships

Create a relationship between tables

In the previous exercise you have created a relationship between two tables by allowing these to share a common field, the ni_number. You can create relationships between tables even though the names of the fields are different. For example, assume that you want to create another table called course table. In this table you have a list of courses that you offer. Lecturers teach these courses and this is done in particular weeks. Therefore there should be a link between the new course table and both previous tables, i.e. the lecturer and contact_hours tables.

We first create the course table as shown below. Notice that the course has a lecturer_id field to identify who is teaching on the course. This field will need to be linked to the lecturer table in order to avoid data redundancy. (Duplicating data within as well as across tables)

	Field Name	Data Type
🔑	course_number	Text
	course_name	Text
	lecturer_id	Number
	week_number	Number

course : Table

To create relationships between tables select the relationships option from the main menu. This is found under the tools button.

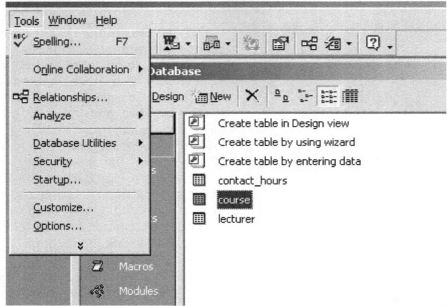

Select each table that you want in the relationship and this will bring up a list in the relationship window. Drag the field from the table that you want to link from into the table that you want to link to. Here I drag the lecturer_id from course table to ni_number field in the lecturer table. This creates a relationship which is identified by the menu at the bottom right of the figure. By clicking create the relationship between tables is created.

48

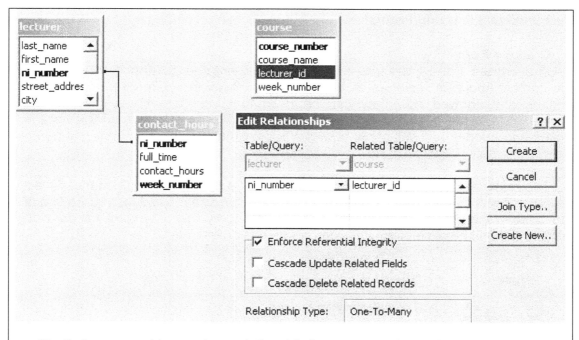

Similarly we need to create a relationship between week numbers in course table and contact_hours table. The resulting relationship diagram is shown below.

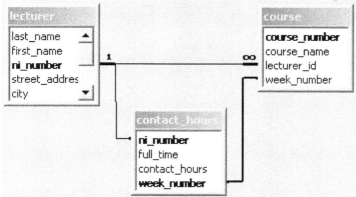

These are very simple examples, but they should serve as starters towards you becoming an expert at creating relationships between tables.

Exercise 3.5. Using Forms

Create a Form
In exercises 1 and 2 we created the tables and entered the data that represents the contact hours for lecturers and the relevant information. Exercise 3 introduced queries and showed how they can be used to create a dynaset of data that corresponds to the criteria described in the query. Forms help to organise data in tables and queries and will show how this is done next. Once again this will be an overview simply to demonstrate the principles.

To create a form; select the Forms button on the right of the main menu. Select new and the options that are available for creating forms are listed for you. Notice at the bottom that you have to select the table or query that you want the form to correspond to. I have selected the lecturer table as an example.

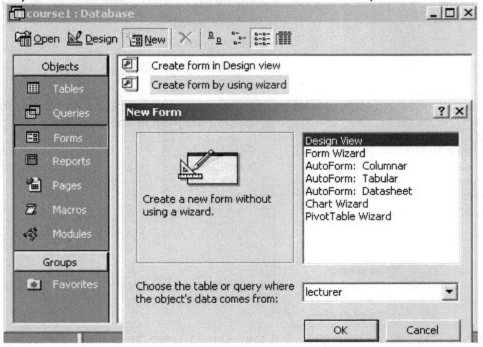

Perhaps the easiest way to create a form is by using the autoform options. There are three of these listed and you can try each one to see the forms that they create. Do not save these since you are only trying to familiarise yourself with the options.

I have selected columnar autoform type and this is shown below. Notice that you can use the arrow at the bottom of the form to scroll through the records; here record 1 of 4 is displayed.

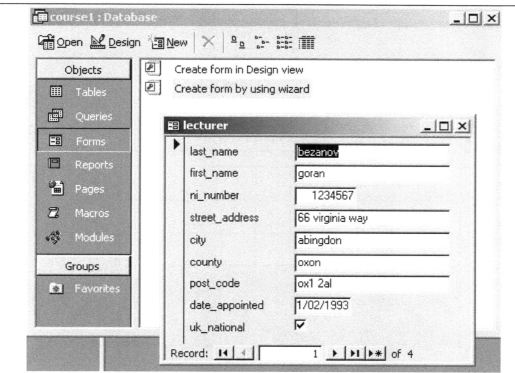

You can use the form to add new entries to the table. For example assume that another lecturer called Michael Jordan has been appointed. To add this entry in the form you use the new button create icon at the bottom of the form (marked with an astrix *).

This causes a blank form to be displayed where you can enter the data.

After you have saved the form you can open the lecturer table in datasheet view to confirm that the new record has been included.

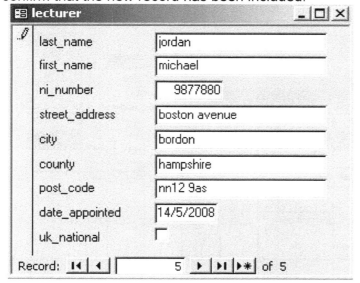

Creating forms in design view.

Sometimes the standard form templates are not adequate for the data that we want to display and in this case we can design our own form in design view. To do this you need to select create form in design view and once again you have to select the table or query that it applies to.

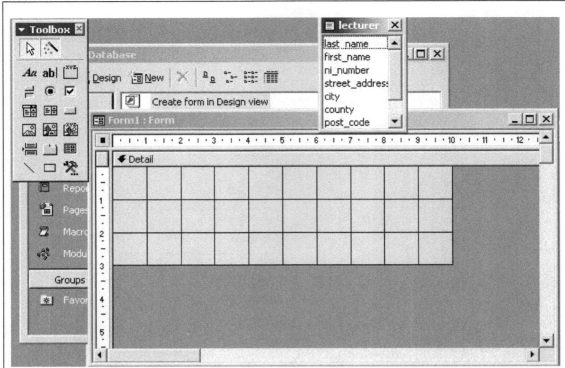

Notice that the fields, which are in the lecturer table, are displayed in a small window in top right corner. The tools menu bar on the left helps you to create the graphical objects to use in the form. The approach to form design is to select the tool from the toolbar menu and to associate it with a field in the table. For example let us design a form to include the last name field.

To do this select the last_name from the list on lecturer field box and drag it to the form in the place that you want it to be. Repeat for all the other fields that you wish to include in the form. I saved my form as form 1 and it ended up looking like this.

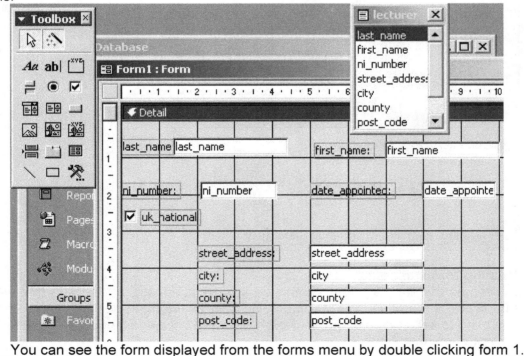

You can see the form displayed from the forms menu by double clicking form 1.

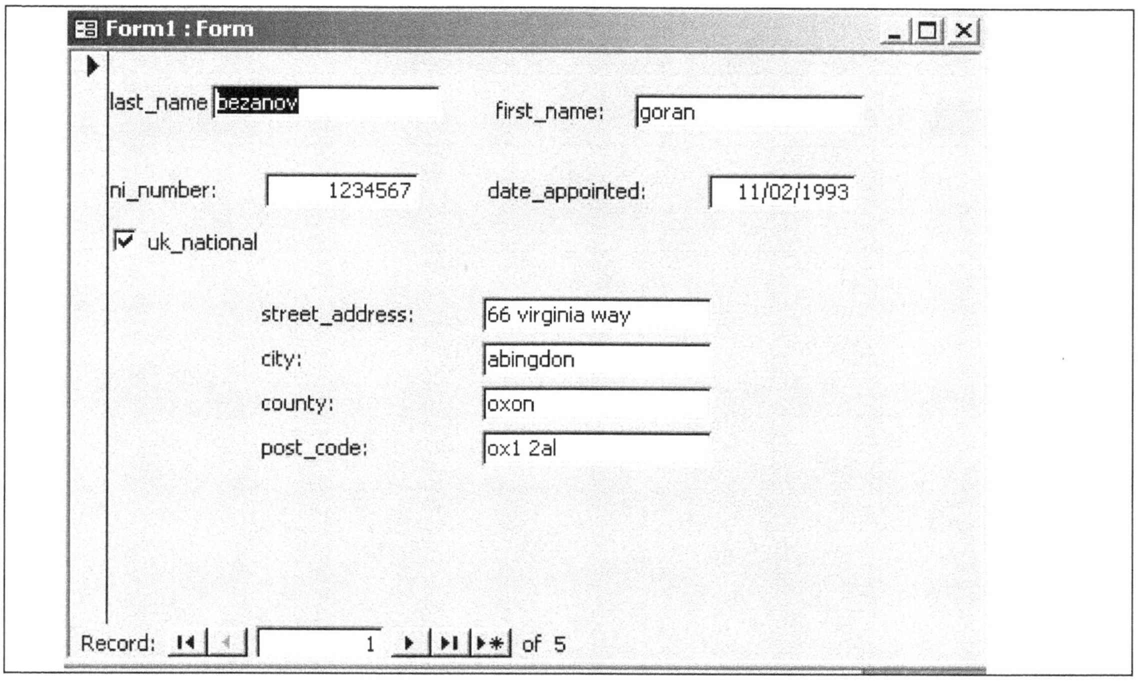

Form1 : Form

last_name: bezanov   first_name: goran

ni_number: 1234567   date_appointed: 11/02/1993

☑ uk_national

street_address: 66 virginia way
city: abingdon
county: oxon
post_code: ox1 2al

Record: 1 of 5

Exercise 3.6. Creating reports

Using reports

Creating reports is very similar in nature to the way that we create forms. From the main menu you select the reports button and once again by clicking new a series of options are listed. In design view you choose your own layout and move the fields onto the place in the report that you want then displayed. You create labels in the report by selecting the text button [A] from the toolbar and drawing the text box where you want it to be. Each label in the report that you create is written in the form. For example, you want the header of the report to say that 'This report shows which lecture has worked during the various weeks'. You select the text button [A] and create a text box in the header section. You can size it by using the mouse to stretch the box to fit the form.

To add data to the form you drag the relevant field into the location of the report where you want it to appear. This is repeated for every field and also where required you can add a text box to describe the field. My example report structure is shown below.

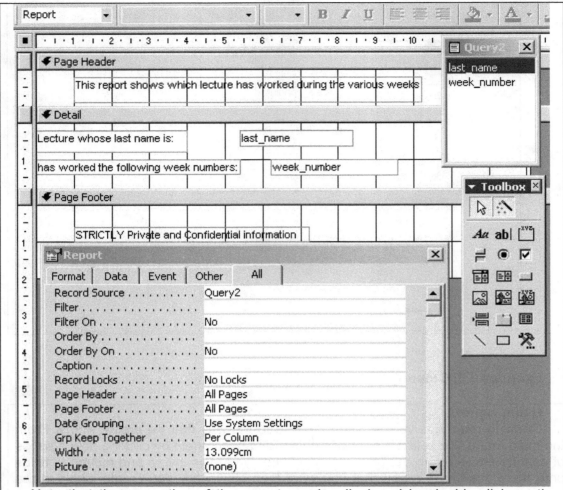

Note that the properties of the report can be displayed by double-click on the object selected. At the bottom of the figure you can see the properties of the report. By selecting different labels, the properties of these will be displayed.

When the report is generated the data fields and labels that you have designed will appear in the report that is ready to print. The report produced in my design is very simple and looks like this.

This report shows which lecture has worked during the various weeks

Lecture whose last name is: bezanov

has worked the following week numbers: 1

Lecture whose last name is: elvis

has worked the following week numbers: 1

Lecture whose last name is: mohamed

has worked the following week numbers: 1

Lecture whose last name is: sarah

has worked the following week numbers: 1

STRICTLY Private and Confidential information

Once again there are many other features that will help you to produce more creative reports but the above simply serves as an example.

CHAPTER 4 DATABASE DESIGN

4.1. Database design considerations

Designing an efficient database application requires much thought and as with everything else, you improve with experience. In this section I will give you some basic ideas to start you off, but you will need to look elsewhere after you have mastered the basics. [1,2,3] You begin a design by identifying the scope of the database. The scope defines what the database will contain. For example, if you are designing a database for a college that will store information about lecturers and their contact hours, then your scope has to encompass all the data that you consider important. In chapter 3 we produced two tables as examples of lecturer information that could be used to define the scope of the database. Thus in this case we limit the scope to the entities of lecturers and their contact hours along with the attributes associated with these entities. If this is all the information that we want, then we do not need anything else. This idea of limiting the scope to only the necessary data is very important because many database users want everything in their database, just in case they need it. By including information that, although relevant, is not necessary would result in scope-less projects that are prone to failure. Therefore the scope of the database describes the relevant information that it must contain.

4.2. Normalisation

The goal of all database projects is to organise the data efficiently. Once again, consider the example of lecturers and their contact hours. You could store all the data in a single table, like a spreadsheet. For each week you could store the lecturers that are teaching that week and their information as well as the detail about contact hours. Figure 4.1 shows an example of how this data could be arranged.

Notice from Figure 4.1 that quite a lot of the information is repeated. For example, Elvis Price has taught in weeks 1, 2 and 3 and therefore all his information is repeated for each of these weeks. When data is repeated in a table it is called redundant. This repetition of data also consumes memory for data storage and this in turn causes database searches to become less efficient. In the example of Figure 4.1, to reduce data redundancy it would be necessary to create a new table called contact hours and link it to the lecturer_table as we have done in the examples of Chapter 3.

To avoid redundancy database design uses normalisation. There are two goals of the normalisation process:
- Eliminating redundant data
- Only storing related data in a table

These goals reduce the amount of space a database consumes and ensure that data is logically stored. This impacts on the efficiency of the database and also the ability to maintain it. To help us design efficient databases the he database community has identified the normalisation rules. These are simple guidelines that must be followed during the design stage so that the final design is as efficient as possible.

last name	first name	ni number	street address	city	county	post_code	date appointed	uk national	full time	contact hours	week number
bezanov	goran	1234567	66 virginia way	abingdon	oxon	ox1 2al	11/02/1993	Yes	Yes	18	1
elvis	price	3456987	1 memphis drive	uxbridge	middlesex	ux1 1ls	02/05/2008	Yes	No	6	1
sarah	conor	7867646	89 ladbrike grove	london	acton	sw10 1qw	04/05/2000	Yes	No	6	2
mohamed	ali	9876543	2 maddison gardens	london	westminster	sw1 1ab	12/03/2003	No	Yes	14	1
jordan	michael	9877880	boston avenue	bordon	hampshire	nn12 9as	14/05/2008	No	Yes	12	1
elvis	price	3456987	1 memphis drive	uxbridge	middlesex	ux1 1ls	02/05/2008	Yes	No	6	2
elvis	price	3456987	1 memphis drive	uxbridge	middlesex	ux1 1ls	02/05/2008	Yes	No	6	3

Figure 4.1. Example data store for lecturer and contact hours.

The Normal Forms (NF)

Normal forms are guidelines that evolved to guide designers in producing efficient databases. There are three basic forms that are referred to as normal forms and are numbered 1NF, 2NF and 3NF. And referred to as first, second and third normal forms respectively. These stand forms are used throughout the database community and much literature can be found to describe them. [18] I shall briefly outline the general principles behind these normal forms and leave it to the reader to source more detailed information if this becomes necessary.

First normal form (1NF)

The first normal form Normal Form (1NF) states that we must not duplicate data within the same column of a table. This is called the atomicity of a table and tables that comply with this rule are said to be atomic. Each row represents a unique record of that entity and must be different in some way from any other row. So if you notice that any two rows are identical the table is not atomic. We also need to look at columns to ensure that all entries in any column are of the same type. For example, in the column labelled ni_number, only numbers are permitted. By ensuring that this is so, the intersection of each row and column should contain only one value which is not repeated. If your table is not atomic in this way, then you would have to create a separate table to store the information that is repeated. In order to access the data and make your design compliant, you would create a relationship between these two tables. Note that the information that was repeated would now be stored only in the newly created table. That is to say, it is not necessary to store the information in both tables because we have established a relationship between them.

For example consider the data in Figure 4.2. In our lecturer_table we have decided to introduce separate columns for the courses that each lecturer teaches. This is done by adding columns to the right of the table. There are five possible courses that each lecturer can teach but only courses one and two are shown for convenience.

last name	first name	ni number	street address	city	county	post code	date appointed	uk national	course 1	course 2
bez	goran	1234567	66 virginia way	abingdon	oxon	ox1 2al	11/02/1993	Yes	A1	A2
elvis	price	3456987	1 memphis drive	uxbridge	middlesex	ux1 1ls	02/05/2008	Yes	A2	0
sarah	conor	7867646	89 ladbrike grove	london	acton	sw10 1qw	04/05/2000	Yes	A3	0
mo	ali	9876543	2 addison gardens	london	westminster	sw1 1ab	12/03/2003	No	A4	A2
jordan	mike	9877880	boston avenue	bordon	hampshire	nn12 9as	14/05/2008	No	A5	A4

Figure 4.2 1NF example of non-compliance

Looking at Figure 4.2 we recall the rules imposed by 1NF: eliminate duplicate rows from the same table. There are no identical rows and so there is no duplicity here. Looking at the columns, we also note that all data are of the correct type. Therefore it seems that our table is 1NF compliant. Note however that some lecturers only teach one course. Therefore, if a lecturer only teaches one course the column labelled course 2 is not necessary in his record. In the event that there is a significant variation in the courses that lecturers teach, having redundant fields would make the database inefficient. In that case it would make sense to create another table to store the courses, and this table would have a relationship with the lecturer_team table. As a result neither table would contain empty fields. Furthermore, imagine the case where a lecturer already teaches two courses, and then decides that they want to start teaching on a new course. The table would need to be modified to include another column for course 3. This will introduce more empty fields on account of lecturers that are not teaching on the new course. As a consequence there would be columns with a large number of recurring null fields. To avoid this it is sensible to introduce another table to store the courses information. The relationship between the lecturer and course would need to be a 1:M relationship and this would make the design 1NF compliant. Therefore looking at Figure 4.2, we could deduce that columns for course 1 and course 2 are not 1NF compliant because of the large number of repeating null fields in columns for courses.

It can be seen from this simple example that the decision about the number of tables and their attributes is made as the design progresses. In the above it is clear that new tables need to be introduced because data is repeated in columns of the existing table. Thus 1NF compliance is guiding our choice of tables during our design.

Second normal form (2NF)
The statement that describes 2NF is to remove subsets of data that apply to multiple rows of a table and place them in separate tables. This means that subsets rather than whole record are repeated. In this manner 2NF is an extension of 1NF

designed to further reduce data redundancy. An example of this was in the case we considered in Figure 4.1 where Elvis Price and all the details were repeated because he taught in weeks 1,2 and 3. Here a subset of the record was repeated rather than the whole record. In that example, we created a new table called contact_hours and established relationships between tables through the use of foreign keys. (Refer to Chapter 3 exercises.)

Therefore it is seen that 2NF attempts to reduce the amount of redundant data in a table by extracting it, placing it in new table(s) and creating relationships between those tables.

Third normal form (3NF)

For a database to comply with 3NF the following requirements have to be satisfied,

- Already meet the requirements of both 1NF and 2NF
- Remove columns that are not fully dependent upon the primary key.

Consider again the lecturer table as an example. The list of attributes is as follows.

- last name
- first name
- ni number
- street address
- city
- county
- post code
- date appointed
- uk national

For 3NF compliance the first requirement is that the table must satisfy the requirements of 1NF and 2NF. There are no duplicate columns in the lecturer table and we have the primary key (ni_number). Therefore the lecturer table is 1NF compliant. There is no data redundancy because data subsets are not duplicated in the table. Therefore the table is also 2NF compliant.

To ensure 3NF compliance we must check to see if all of the columns are fully dependent upon the primary key. In our example, the primary key is the ni_number and we must analyse each of the fields to see if they are fully dependent on this primary key. If you do the analysis you will find that all the fields are dependent on the primary key and so the database is 3NF compliant.

For the sake of argument let us assume that the lecturer table is non-3NF compliant. To do this we add some more fields to illustrate that these do not depend on the primary key. Assume that two more fields are added to the lecturer table. The hourly rate, which is how much we pay the lecturer per hour, and the total weekly pay. Looking at these attributes we can see that the information is necessary. We want to know how much we are paying each lecturer and so the hourly rate is needed for each lecturer. This will be dependent on the primary key. However the total weekly pay can be calculated by simple multiplication of hours worked that week and the hourly rate. As a result total pay is not fully dependent on the primary key. Therefore it should be removed from the table, so that the table can be 3NF compliant.

From these considerations it transpires that good database design must be matched with good table structures. In good database design we wish to avoid data anomalies/redundancies by controlling the table structure logically. The process of identifying and eliminating data anomalies and redundancies is called normalisation. The above are only brief descriptions and additional reading on normalisation can be found elsewhere. [1,2,19]

4.3.　Basic database design steps

Having considered the rules of normalisation we need to identify the approach to database design.　Depending on where you are employed as a database designer, you will be expected to follow design procedures adopted by the employer. Many software houses use dedicated software design tools (CASE tools) for their database development and you would be expected to learn how to use these. However, assuming that you do not have any CASE tools the general approach to design is outlined here in a number of steps.

- **Step 1:** Obtain requirements specification. This covered in more detail in chapter 5 of this text.
- **Step 2:** Draw system context. This is the original model of the system that is used as a starting point for design.
- **Step 3:** Identify the entities in from the specification and use these to decide on the tables that you need. Use the Nouns in the specification to help you to identify the entities.
- **Step 4:** Describe attributes of each entity, to avoid data redundancy do not include a field if it can be calculated from other fields. Designate a primary key for each table. Use the adjectives in the specification to help you to identify the attributes.
- **Step 5:** Describe the relationships between the entities and designate the foreign keys to reflect these relationships.
- **Step 6:** Normalise the tables

4.4.　Requirement specification

The starting point of every design project is to obtain the requirements specification. There are formal descriptions of specifications and some of these are described in Chapter 5 that deals with project management. However, in the context of designing a simple database application the initial specification will consist of a client brief. This brief will then be expanded upon with consultation between the client and the developer and this is done over a period of time.

Assume that your initial client brief is as follows: (This brief is slightly modified in relation to previous version)

MIG Consulting Ltd has contacted you to create a conceptual model for a database solution to reflect the requirements for its training program. The client brief is as follows.

MIG Consulting Ltd provides IT training services to corporations in Linux and Cisco systems. The engage a team of trainers to visit the client premises and deliver on-site, hands-on training.　MIG Consulting Ltd pays each team a pre-arranged fee for their services.

- There are a number of teams of lecturers that deliver IT training.
- The company engages each team to train a particular course at a particular location.
- Each team consists of lecturers who are trained to deliver a particular course. This can be only one course per lecturer.
- Courses are taught at different locations.

This just an example of a client brief from which requirement specification needs to be derived, but it is a good starting point for designing the database. From these we can generate the context diagram.

Context diagram

Context diagrams are used to define the boundary between the system that is being developed and external entities that interact with the system (i.e. its environment). Therefore, in database design the focus is on the interfaces that the system needs to have between entities. These entities are represented by named boxes and connected using directional arrows. My context diagrams always have a central block that represents my system, which connects to other blocks that have interfaces to it which are represented by arrows. Therefore, my context diagram for this example could be as shown in Figure 4.3.

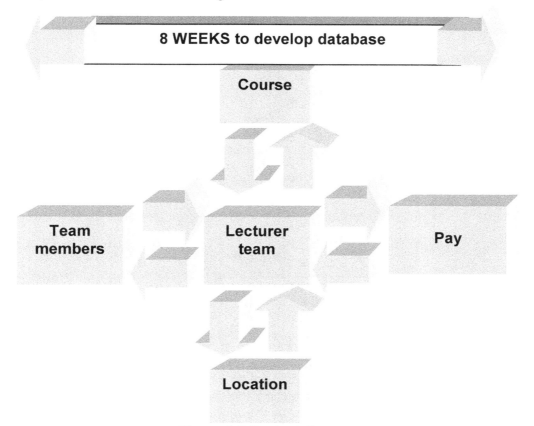

Figure 4.3 Context diagram

The important thing to note is that the context diagram is produced early on and as I spend more time on the project, things will become clearer, so that I may refine my design. In Figure 4.3, I have identified the main components of the database that I need to design. I have teams consisting of lecturers who teach on courses, which are at different locations and they are paid as a team for the training that they deliver. This means that I have five boxes representing five entities. There may be more entities later due to normalisation and other design issues, but these will suffice for now. I know that the boxes are related, but I am not sure how, so I include bi-directional arrows to represent relationships. To help me with project planning I also identify the timescale that I have to complete the project.

The context diagram would normally be extended to subsystems and subcomponents. This is to say that the boxes representing entities in Figure 4.3 can be broken down into smaller sections at a later stage, but the context diagram should be simple and only needs to identify the main components and the relationship between these.

It is worth noting that the context diagram of Figure 4.3 is fairly simple in that there are only five entities. In a more elaborate project, with more entities, the context diagram would also become more elaborate. In these projects the context diagram would use full lined arrows to describe information flow and dashed line arrows to describe any controls. A hypothetical example is shown in Figure 4.4. Here a part of a student record system is shown.

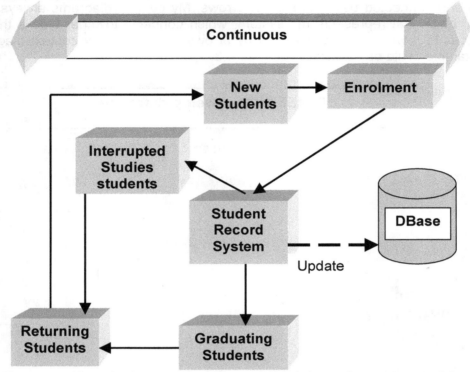

Figure 4.4 Hypothetical context diagram with information and control flows

This system needs to record information about students that are currently attending courses. The information flow is shown between the various subsystems and the main system. For example, control flow is shown as a dashed lined arrow to the database because there is an action that needs to be performed. Namely the database needs to be updated with the appropriate information whenever any changes are made. This is an over-simplified example, used mainly to show the concept of information flow and control flow. The context diagram should be as simple and as clear as possible because it usually serves to define an approach to manage the project. If the initial context is correct then the subsequent stages of project management will become more manageable.

4.5.   Database design example

Defining tables, attributes and relationships
Steps 3, 4 and 5 are considered at the same design stage because they define the way that data is organised in the database. While we are considering these steps we also keep in mind the rules on normalisation. This design process is iterative and as the design progresses new tables are created in order to satisfy the requirements or business rules that are outlined in the specification. Perhaps the best way to proceed is by providing an example design of the lecturer database.

In my context diagram I have identified the five entities that I need in my design. These are, lecturer team, course, location, hours_worked and pay. These should be sufficient to begin my design. We know that there are relationships between entities and also that each entity has attributes.

Taking a closer look at these entities we attempt to establish relationships between them. In particular we look for one-to-many relationships between entities. The relationship between these entities must be established in tables, and can be done by using a foreign key. We also look for many-to-many relationships between entities, because in this case there is the need for a third entity that associates the two entities in the relationship. (See Chapter 2 on ERD composite entity).

When we are looking at attributes of each entity we are at the same time identifying the attribute that is unique to the entity that we can designate as the primary key. If we think of entities as nouns and we list the adjectives that describe the nouns, these are the attributes, which become the fields in the table. Thus for example, the attributes of the lecturer_team entity are team_id, team_contact_number, and team_fees. No two teams have the same team_id so this can be the primary key for the table. Figure 4.5 shows the lecturer_team table and its fields: team_id, team_contact_number, team_fees and the data type of each field is also shown. Figure 4.6 shows example record in the lecturer_team table. Note that the team_id is the primary key and that other fields such as fee and contact number may not be unique for every record and so they are not considered for primary key choice.

Table Name: lecturer_team

Field	Data Type
team_id (primary key)	Text
team_contact_number	Text
team_fees	Currency

Figure 4.5 The lecturer_team table and its fields

team_id (primary key)	team_contact_number	team_fees
linux_trainers	0207 1234567	£500
cisco_trainers	0208 7890123	£400

Figure 4.6 Example records in the lecturer_team table

At this point, you might ask why team member would not be an attribute of team_id. Since each team can have an arbitrary number of members, you do know how many fields to allocate. If there were two members to a team then only two fields could be used, namely member_1 and member_2. But if another team had four members, then a total of four fields need to be allocated to all the records. The team that only has two members will have empty fields. Therefore, you do not know how many fields to allocate to the team_id table for members. If you were to allocate a specific number of fields, some of which are empty for some teams, then the table would not comply with the 1NF as discussed earlier. This implies that we need another entity to describe team members. Therefore, we create a team_member entity with the attributes member_name, team_id, course, and contact_number. The team_member table and its fields are shown in Figure 4.7. Notice that this table includes team_id as a foreign key in order to set up a relationship with the lecturer_team table. This establishes a relationship between a lecturer and the team that they belong to. The foreign key is not unique for each record and therefore another key, namely member_name is used as the primary key.

Table Name: team_member

Field	Data Type
member_name (primary key)	Text
team_id (foreign key)	Text
course	Text
contact_number	Text

Figure 4.7. The team_member table and its fields

Example records in the team_member table are shown in Figure 4.8. Note that no two members have the same name and therefore it is appropriate to use this field as the primary key.

member_name (primary key)	team_id	course	contact_number
Goran Bezanov	Cisco_101	C_100	0867 123456
Elvis Price	Cisco_101	C_200	1024 123987
Sarah Conor	Cisco_101	C_300	0996 567987
Mo Ali	Linux_292	L_995	0844 549834
Mike Jordan	Linux_292	L_996	0789 700675

Figure 4.8 Records in the team_member table

Note that I have included the course that each lecturer is teaching, as a field in the team_member table. This is because the business rules state that each lecturer is trained to deliver a single course. If the rules were changed and a lecturer allowed to teach on more than one course then this field would not comply with 2NF. Therefore, if it is assumed that each lecturer can only teach on one course, then the course field can be used to describe a team member. To clarify this, note that we have already defined the foreign key to relate lecturers to their teams. We could also say that courses need to be in a new table, but since each lecturer teaches only one course, this action is not necessary. You could also remove the course field from the team_member table and put it into the lecturer_team table. This would not affect the database structure as far as normalisation is concerned.

For the team_member table we defined a primary key by considering the fields that make each record unique in the table. Course and team_id are shared between records so the only options for the primary key are the contact_number and member_name. We could of course introduce another field such as member_id which would be unique, but for convenience let us assume that no the names of team members are unique, and no two lecturers have identical names. Therefore member_name is selected as the primary key. Alternatively, contact_number could be the primary key if it could be assumed that no two members share the same telephone number.

Note that we have included team_id in the team_member table. This is also used in the lecturer_team table. It therefore serves to relate the two tables and declaring the team_id as a foreign key in the team_member table does this. This makes sense because teams are engaged in delivering the training and these teams are made up of lecturers. If a lecturer were allowed to belong to more than one team then the table would not comply with 2NF.

Another way to think about this involves the cardinality of the relationship between lecturer_team and team_member. This is a one-to-many relationship: One lecturer_team has many team_members, but each team_member is in just one lecture_team. Therefore it makes sense to use the team_id as a foreign key to set up a relationship with the lecturer_team table. By using this relationship the two tables can combine to retrieve data relating to lecturer_team details, team members involved and the courses that these lecturers teach.

Location is another entity that we have identified, because we need to keep track of where the teams are lecturing. This can vary by location and so we create the location table. The attributes of the entity location are location_name, address, contact_name, contact_number, fee, and team_id. For example, the table called location with its fields is shown in Figure 4.9.

Table Name: location

Field Name	Data Type
Location_name (primary key)	Text
Address	Text
Contact_name	Text
Contact_number	Text
Fee	Currency
Team_id	text

Figure 4.9. The location table and its fields

For this table example records are shown in Figure 4.10. Here it is seen that the teams are engaged at two distinct locations. The team_id identifies the teams and the other details relate to the location. In this case team_id is used as a foreign key to define a relationship between the location and team member tables. Notice that there is no relationship between location and lecturer tables, but because there are relationships between lecture_team⇒team_member and team_member⇒location, it is implicit that you could obtain information about the lecturers that are teaching at a particular location.

Location_name (primary key)	Address	Contact _name	Contact _number	Fee	Team_id (foreign key)
Gullivers	43 Pall Mall	Sandra Lee	0207 465734	£800	Cisco_101
Microsoft	17 Abbey Road	Mick Jag	0207 989466	£900	Linux_292

Figure 4.10. Example records in the location table

At this point you might notice that contact_number field appears with the same name in all of three tables that we have created. However, in each case it is a different contact number pertaining to a different record. Thus although the name of the field is the same there is no direct relationship between these fields in the different tables. In other words you are allowed to use the same name across different tables and unless you specifically relate these by using a foreign key, they will not interfere with each other.

Note also that the fee charged to the customer is not the same as the fee paid to the lecturer_team because MIG Consulting Ltd wants to make a profit. Therefore the two fields are separate. On the other hand, if the fee paid to lecturer_team were a fixed percentage of the fees charged to the client, then team_fees in the lecturer_team table would not comply with 3NF. That is to say the team_fee in this case is not fully dependent on the primary key in the lecturer_team table because it can be calculated from the fee charged to the client. Note also that we have included team_id field in the location table. This is a foreign key that has also been used as a foreign key in the team_member table. Thus it is seen that the same field can be used as a foreign key in more than one table. This means that the particular field is shared by a number of tables, and this perfectly admissible.

Looking back at the context diagram there are two more entities that we need to describe namely the pay and the course entities. We have to ask ourselves if both of these are necessary. Course and the amount paid to teams have already been defined as attributes of the team_member table. Fees charged to customers are defined in the location table. All these fields comply with the rules on normalisation and therefore it is not necessary to create separate tables for these. This consideration is important in database design because you should not include in your design more tables than necessary.

Thus far we have defined the entities describing the business of delivering courses. We have to ask ourselves if this is all that we need to make a working database. Looking at the context diagram we have defined all the components and so we should be ready to implement the database. But we notice that there is no mention in our design how the booking is made for a course. We have contact details but presumably some record needs to be kept about the booking of a team of lecturers to deliver training at a given location. This shows that the context diagram that we produced in the beginning is not complete and that we need another entity. This does not mean that we were wrong in the first context diagram, it was a good starting point, and as we progress through the design we are free to introduce modifications to the context diagram. Therefore it appears that we need another table called booking. The attributes of this entity can be discerned by describing the process of booking a training course. Let us consider the booking transaction next.

We know that the MIG Consulting Ltd books a specific lecturer_team to deliver a specific course at a specified location for a specified fee. We also note that courses are booked for specific dates and that they start and end at specific times and this is arranged in discussions with the client. From this information, the attributes of the booking entity are team_id, location, date, start_time, end_time and fee. The booking table and its fields are shown in Figure 4.11.

Table Name: Booking

Field Name	Data Type
Team_id	Text
location	Text
Date	Date/Time
Start_time	Date/Time
End_time	Date/Time
Fee	Currency

Figure 4.11. The booking table and its fields

Assume that the bookings table contains the records shown in Figure 4.12. When we make a booking we need to book a location for a team to deliver a course for a specific fee. For this reason each of these fields is used as a foreign key in the table. It must be said that each of these is a foreign key to a different table. Typically you would not need more than one foreign key to the same table. I hope that this is not confusing, because the above Figure 4.11 shows three foreign keys. This is not a problem if these keys point to different tables. In our example of Figure 4.11 the fee and the location are both fields in the location table. You might argue that it is not necessary to have two keys point to the same table because in each case they are linked to the primary key of that table. By linking to the primary key of that table you could uniquely identify both the location and the fee. Nevertheless, it is permissible to have more than one foreign key form the same table if this makes the design more transparent and data easier to follow.

Either way it should be clear that by specifying foreign keys, all records in that table are uniquely identified through the foreign key relationship to other tables. If this still does not make sense, think of a table that contains the fees that a location attracts. A booking table needs to know this and so the field in the booking table called fee is a foreign key from the location table. If the fee for the location changes in the location table, then this propagates directly to the bookings table through the explicitly defined foreign key relationship. Were this relationship not explicitly defined, the fees associated with the booking could still be obtained if the primary key from the locations table was used as the foreign key in the bookings table. But this would be indirect, and you would need an update query to make the necessary changes to the fees.

Team_id (foreign key)	Location (foreign key)	Date	Start_time	End_time	Fee (foreign key)
Cisco_101	Gullivers	21/05/09	9:00	12:30	£800
Linux_292	Microsoft	21/05/09	9:00	12:30	£900
Linux_292	Embassy	31/08/09	14:00	17:30	£500
Cisco_101	Gullivers	31/08/09	14:00	17:30	£800
Cisco_101	Embassy	31/08/09	9:00	12:30	£550

Figure 4.12 Records in the booking table

Next we need to identify the primary key for the booking table. Note that each of the fields has repeating values. This means that no single field uniquely identifies a record in the table. We could generate another field and call it booking_id and this would solve the problem. In fact it is always good to have a booking reference number because these are planned in advance. The alternative, if you do not want to create another field is to define a compound key from the available fields. We look at the fields and try to identify those which combine to make the record unique. One team can only be in one location at any one time, so a combination of these three fields can be used to uniquely describe a record. That is team_id + location + start_time could be used as a unique compound key for the bookings table.

Now that the tables have been identified you need to check for normalisation and apply the rules for 1Nf, 2NF and 3NF. You can do this as an exercise and make any corrections as necessary. You can discern from the foregoing that good database design is very much down to experience and a clear understanding of the problems associated with data redundancy and anomalies. The best way to improve is to practice until you develop your skills so that database design becomes almost intuitive.

4.6. Chapter summary

In this chapter we covered the basic rules of database design. Normalisation is a commonly accepted approach to ensuring that the tables are designed efficiently. The three normal forms, 1NF, 2NF and 3NF are useful guidelines to efficient design. All design starts with a requirement specification and this is covered briefly. Context diagram is useful as a starting point and this can be used to identify entities in your design. Some basic rules are given as a guideline and this is followed though with an example design. The example given is very basic and it serves to show how tables are selected and relationships between the tables are defined to show how data can be linked between tables.

Exercises

4.1 Explain how normal forms are used in database design.

4.2 What is a context diagram?

4.3 Draw a context diagram for the following database design projects,
  i. Car rental agency
  ii. A school library
  iii. Your own accounting database

4.4 How would you normally identify entities and their attributes in database design applications?

4.5 For the example design covered in this chapter perform the following tasks,
  a. Normalisation check on the tables
  b. Draw an ERD model for the design
  c. In the ERD model identify the composite entities

4.6 Design a database for the following businesses,
  a. Car rental agency
  b. A school library
  c. Your own accounting database

4.7 Which of the following tables complies with 1NF

4.8 The following table describes a collection of data stored as a spreadsheet. Design a normalised database to store the same data

last name	first name	street address	city	county	post code	salary	department	line manager
bez	goran	66 virginia way	abingdon	oxon	ox1 2al	1000	ECCE	leon
elvis	price	1 memphis drive	uxbridge	middlesex	ux1 1ls	2000	ECCE	leon
sarah	conor	89 ladbrike grove	london	acton	sw10 1qw	1000	ESD	mike
mo	ali	2 maddison gardens	london	westminster	sw1 1ab	1000	ESD	sara
jordan	mike	boston avenue	bordon	hampshire	nn12 9as	2000	ECCE	jo
john	conor	89 ladbrike grove	london	acton	sw10 1qw	1000	ECCE	jo

CHAPTER 5 DATABASE PROJECT PLANNING

5.1. Introduction

Project management is a very broad discipline and there are a large number of resources that can be accessed on–line as well as in published literature. [20] [21] In a general sense it concerns the management of resources in order to deliver the desired results. Resources can be: people, software tools, premises, IT and communications, hardware, finance, administration, marketing etc. The project deliverable could be: software or hardware products, services, training, customer service and relations, new product development etc. A very important element of project management is the delegation of responsibility for the project. Depending on the size of the project, the levels of responsibility will vary but in a very general sense it has to be said that all projects should identify persons that are responsible at every stage in the project. For a start every project must have a project manager, who is responsible for performing the following tasks,

- **Plan the Project:** Very simply stated, a good plan saves time and reduces the cost of the project. Or, alternatively defined, a bad plan costs time and money, reduces profit and can easily result in a loss and/or bankruptcy.

- **Estimate the Cost and Establish the Budget**: Budget is a very important factor since it establishes the limits to which costs can be taken. Ultimately cost is the driving factor behind the majority of resources that are needed in a project.

- **Identify and Acquire Necessary Resources:** (hardware equipment, software, people skills etc.) Resources that are needed in a project need to be resourced during the planning stages so that costs can be determined.

- **Manage the project:** (to the schedule and within budget): Not everything can be planned. There are always potential problems that cannot be foreseen. Contingency plans need to be in place in order to mitigate the effects of unforeseen problems.

Managing a project typically involves a number of stages. As projects vary so the project management approach will have to be modified to suit them, but in general project management can be divided into the stages given in Figure 5.1. These stages will be describe briefly next.

As seen in Figure 5.1 there are a number of stages in the life cycle of a project.

Project definition

This involves establishing the requirements, which will serve to guide all the other stages of the project. For example, a requirements document will be used to plan the activity, model any proposed solutions and evaluate these. Requirements will be needed during the implementation stage as well as commissioning. Thus, it is seen that a significant amount of effort is needed to accurately establish the project requirements. The next stage in Figure 5.1 is project planning.

Planning

This is necessary to establish a timed relationship between the available resources and the project deliverables. Typically a project would be broken down into a number of tasks and each of these will be allocated the resources that are needed. Typically timescales will be associated with each task so that progress can be monitored. This is so that each of the tasks can be done relatively autonomously which means that for example different teams could be allocated to different tasks.

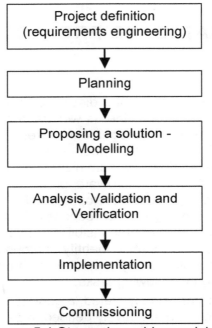

Figure 5.1 Stages in problem solving

Proposing a solution and modelling

Modelling is a resource that can potentially identify problems that are not easy to spot during the planning phase. Additionally, by identifying these problems before the implementation stage, modelling can save time and reduce costs. In general modelling helps to identify project dynamics that would otherwise be difficult or expensive to obtain. When all the models have been completed the proposed solution to the can be identified.

Validation and verification

Following on in Figure 5.1, after the modelling stage there follows a stage during which we need to analyse the proposed solution in order to determine if the solution satisfies the requirements. Validation considers if the proposed solution meets the user requirements as specified in the requirements document. Thus, validation is concerned with answering the question "are we building the correct system"? Verification on the other hand considers whether the system is being built in a correct way. That is to say, verification concerns the analysis from the planning and execution point of view rather than the functional perspective. In the event that either of these identifies errors, the project manager will need to address this and apply the required corrective measures.

Implementation

The next stage is the implementation stage. If all the other stages have been completed in a satisfactory manner, then the implementation stage should be quite straightforward. If, not then problems will occur that will require a return to some of the previous stages, even as far back as the requirements stage. It is of fundamental importance that all the possible errors have been rectified before this stage is reached. If a design error is built into the implemented system, it could be very difficult to identify and very expensive to correct.

Testing and commissioning

The final stage is commissioning. Here the project is delivered to the client, and it is measured against the original set of agreed requirements. At each stage a document is produced to describe the activities of that particular stage. Some more details on these stages are covered next.

5.2. Requirements engineering

Every project needs to be specified so that the parties involved in the project know what their obligations are and the boundaries of their responsibility. In many cases the parties involved will have different backgrounds and therefore a different perspective on the project. For example, the financier of the project may not appreciate the technical complexity of the task in hand, whist the technical director, may not realise the costs involved in the marketing and distribution of the finished product. As there are varieties of projects, so every project will have a somewhat different approach to requirements specification.

There are a very large number of sources that refer to the different requirements specifications. For example in the area of software development, SRS refers to the software requirement specification document. The IEEE [22] is an excellent source for definitions of system and software specifications. A database applications company that outlines the requirements, which they want clients to satisfy before they are engaged on a project, gives a more practical example. [23] Here the database developers are informing the client about the information that they need in order to undertake a database development project. The requirements are very precise and clearly stated. It is not at all clear how these requirements fit in with the IEEE standards, but nevertheless they serve the purpose of defining the requirements from the client perspective.

Benefits of a requirements specification

A well-researched and precise requirements document will serve to help the smooth running of the project throughout its life cycle. Some areas that this will influence are as follows, [24]

Legal basis: It can serve to establish the basis for agreement between the clients and the suppliers on what the project will provide.

Reduced development effort. A formal requirements document encourages the various concerned parties to consider rigorously all of the requirements before design begins. This helps to reduce effort in subsequent redesign, modifications and retesting. Careful review of the requirements can reveal omissions, misunderstandings, and inconsistencies early in the development cycle when these problems are easier to correct.

Provide a basis for estimating costs and schedules. The description of the product to be developed can be used as a realistic basis for estimating project costs. This in turn helps both the clients and the suppliers because they can both make business decision based on this.

Provide a baseline for validation and verification. Project can be validated much more easily if a good requirement document is in place.

Although mainly dealing with software engineering, Somerville gives a very good treatment of requirement analysis. [25] Here, the desirable characteristics of requirements specifications given in are as follows. Requirements specifications should be: [25]

- **Complete**: specification must precisely define all the situations that can be anticipated and the manner of the response to these.
- **Consistent**: there is no conflict between individual requirement statements.
- **Unambiguous**: A statement of a requirement is unambiguous if it can only be interpreted one way.
- **Modifiable**: Statements that are related must be grouped together and those that are not, must be separated. Arranging the requirements document into a logical structure can help with this.

- **Ranked**: Statements are ranked according to their importance in the organisational structure.
- **Testable**: It should be possible for all statements in the requirements specification to be tested according to a pass or fail criteria. If this is not possible, then alternative, quantifiable assessment criteria should be identified.

Even though the above relate primarily to software requirements specifications, they are very general and can therefore be applied to almost any project. That said the above do not really provide us with a way of producing a requirement specification. Within the confines of this text and pertaining to projects that primarily involve science and engineering, the requirements document should be structured according to Table 5.1.

Table 5.1

User requirements	System requirements
Requirements definition: This is the definition of the aims form the user perspective. What is the system or project aiming to achieve? These should be defined to a point where the project can proceed with an acceptable level of risk.	**Requirements definition:** This is the definition of the aims form the system perspective. What is the system or project aiming to achieve? In contrast with user requirements, these should also consider resource implications on system development. (i.e. have we done something like this before?)
Requirements specification: Effectively these are the objectives that need to be met in order that the aims can be satisfied. This will normally consist of functional and Non-Functional requirements as described below.	**Requirements specification:** Objectives as outlined in the user requirements, but from the systems perspective. It should be clear that some objectives would be different when looking at the system as opposed to the user requirements.

As seen in Table 5.1 the requirements document is divided into twp sections. The section on user requirements deals with the functional and non-functional requirements from the user perspective. A somewhat different perspective is the system requirements where the aims consider the system rather than the user. Here the resource implications are taken into account. It is evident that both the user and the system requirements need to be satisfied in order that the project can have a chance of being successfully completed. The functional and non-functional requirements are briefly defined as follows,

Functional requirements: As the name implies, these refer to functions provided by the system for the user. Therefore these requirements are statements that describe how the user and the system are expected to react to particular inputs. In other words functional requirements specify particular behaviours of a user and or a system, or the interaction between these.

Non-functional requirements: These relate to the quality and attempt to quantify the value added components of a system and a user. Generally these will relate to the functional requirements since they operate in the same environment. For, example, if the system is a manufacturing process, and the user is a process operator, then non-functional issues could be the timing constraints on the services or functions offered by the system. On the other hand, if a project were to design a new architecture for a game console, which is based on RISC technology, then the non-functional requirements would include constraints on the development process, standards, etc. Typical non-functional requirements include, reliability, scalability, and cost. It is worth mentioning that because of their qualitative nature these are usually identified using metrics. [26]

The above describes a general template for producing a requirements document for a typical project in science and engineering that are carried out by students at university as part of their course requirements. Please note that this is only a template and the reader is encouraged to consider other sources for further directions. However, the above template is very simple to use and it should provide a solid starting point for specifying project requirements for simple projects.

Figure 5.2 shows the documents that need to be included as part of the requirements engineering process. This is by no means exhaustive, and different projects may need a different set of documents. Nevertheless, the documentation indicated in Figure 5.2 is a useful template to start with, that can be refined as the need arises.

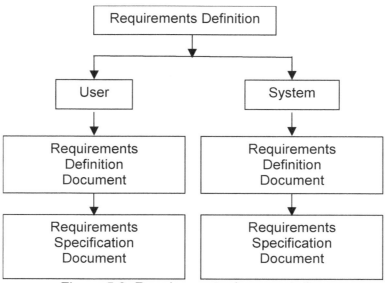

Figure 5.2. Requirements documentation

The components shown in Figure 5.2 are discussed briefly next.

Requirements definition

Perhaps the best place to start with requirements definition is the title of the project. The title for the project can usually be derived from the initial requirements. This initial requirement can originate from a number of sources, such as for example a supervisor, a client, an invitation to tender, an offer of a research grant or from own initiative. In academic research, it is common to arrive at a title after discussions with a professor who will typically be in the position to define the project quite precisely. In the world of politics, you could be asked to by your boss to organise and run a campaign for a candidate in a presidential election. On the other hand in the commercial sector, a manager or a director may ask you to re-organise the department to improve efficiency. In engineering, perhaps your company has just won a contract to build a nuclear power station, and you are going to be the project manager. If you are working as a design engineer for Formula 1, then perhaps your boss has asked you to improve the design of the car so that it performs better in the next season.

It should be clear therefore that there are innumerable ways that we can arrive at the title for a project. As mentioned earlier, research is needed to establish the project aims. Therefore, having arrived at the title how do we begin researching?

The place to begin with research is at the point of ignorance. This is to say that I shall begin at that point where my knowledge about the subject stops. In most cases we will be required to undertake research in the area of our expertise. This saves time and resources, because the person that has been asked to do the research already knows a lot about the subject. But, having said that, recent graduates do not generally have the experience of senior engineers and managers, and when they are asked to do any research, they have to begin at a lower level. There are also implications regarding resources, which are to say, do we have access to the required literature and other resources, such as perhaps literature about a similar project?

Whilst it may be possible in some cases to define project aims without doing any research, it is suggested that the first deliverable in a project is the requirements definition. Research activity that is involved in obtaining a requirement definition typically involves requirement elicitation, analysis, and documentation. From a pragmatic perspective, requirements definition strives for requirements that are good enough to allow the team to proceed with design, construction and testing at an acceptable level of risk.

Requirement specification

Having obtained the requirements definition the next stage is to produce a requirement specification. This entails going into more details in explaining how the requirements definition will be interpreted and implemented.

It has to be said that software requirements specification documents, tend to use requirements specifications to produce a formal document to clear up any ambiguities, omissions and conflicts in the requirements definitions. In non-software projects, the same applies except that it is not necessary or even applicable to use the software model. Within the context of this text, the requirement specification is the refinement of requirements definition to identify the objectives and the steps towards achieving these. The starting point to obtain a requirement specification is to obtain as much information from the client as possible. The initial client brief is a starting point and from this you can decide what other information you need from the client.

A very good example of obtaining the initial details from the client can be found on-line from a database design company. Here the company have produced a website indicating the information that they need the client to provide, so that they can begin drafting a solution. I have included a summary of these here for convenience, but for full details visit the company website. [27]

Aldex Software Limited requirements specification outline:

This is a document that the company is asking the client to provide. It details the information that the company needs in order to consider whether they are able to engage on the project or not. The basic document that is needed is called a Requirements Specification. The following topics should be included in this document.

Introduction;
- Briefly outline your background, Who you are? What you do? What is the business problem you are trying to solve and why you need a new system?

System Overview;
- **Users;** Who is intended to use it, How many users are there (both the total number and the maximum number of concurrent users at any one time)? Are they the same type of user or different (e.g. sales and management), What level or computer experience will the users have (e.g. familiarity with Word/Excel).
- **Current situation**; What have you been using up to now (e.g. paper, nothing, DOS database). Do you have existing data that needs to be converted to the new system? What format is this data in and can it be exported, e.g. to a .csv text file. What main problems do the users have at present? What sort of security (e.g. different group with different access rights) is required? What

hardware/environmental constraints are there. For example, the system is to be run on Windows 2000 machines each with a minimum of 128Mb RAM. What sort of technical support is available in-house.

- Describe what your current back-up regime is (e.g. tape back-up one/day) and if/how you expect the new system to fit in with this. If this is not currently defined then think how much data loss you could suffer. For example would it be a major disaster if you lost the last 30 minutes of work or would you be happy reverting to yesterday's/last week's version?

Design constraints;

- What other systems, if any, will this system integrate/communicate with e.g. export data to a financial system, import data from Excel, etc.
- What external communications are involved e.g. automated faxing, import csv data from FTP site, export data to an accounts system, etc.
- What Business Rules that need to be included, for example maximum credit allowed is 5,000.
- Are there any Business Processes that need to be catered for, e.g. credit card authorisation
- Are there any technical standards that must be complied with, e.g. code must be written using the Leszynski/Reddick naming convention.
- Approx. number of records required initially plus anticipated growth e.g. 1,000 customers increasing at 100 per year; 10,000 jobs increasing at 1,000/year; etc.
- Will remote users need access (e.g. mobile workers with a laptop). If so do they just need a copy of the database on their laptop or will they need to dial-in to the main system to get the most up-to-date information. Will they be updating information in the field for later downloading onto the main system. Any what about other sites?
- Maintainability/future expansion. Include your thoughts on who will maintain the system in future (e.g. in-house), any plans for future developments, etc.
- Any reliability constraints? Acceptable downtime? Can you cope if the system is shut down overnight? For an hour during the day? For a whole day?

Desired system;

- What are you expecting? e.g. Will it be networked or stand-alone system, help files, documentation, full source code, training, support, etc. Detail what is essential and differentiate these from what would be nice. Don't automatically ask for everything unless you really do need it, for example documentation can be very expensive. If you are to maintain the system make sure you state that you require the full source code - alternatively if the developer is to maintain the system you may settle for an escrow agreement (where the source is held by an independent third party).

Functional Requirements

- This section should describe what the system is to accomplish rather than how it is to be accomplished. This should consist of a list, with the most important items at the top. Each entry on the list should be specified in a format similar to the following.
- A description of the requirement. This will probably be a couple of lines explaining what you want to achieve. Make sure that you provide sufficient detail. e.g. Produce a report of spend/department/year on demand with the user selecting the Department and the financial year required (note that you would also need to define how your financial year is calculated!).
- How important is this requirement (essential, preferred, nice to have, not essential, etc).
- Any known design/implementation issues relating to this requirement.

- Does this requirement interact with other requirements.
- Anything else affecting this requirement (e.g. only authorised personnel should have access)

Data to be Held
- Describe what data tables you expect to hold. For example, customer records, contact details, machine records, etc. Provide as much detail as you can. For example a customer record might consist of a name, address, tel. no, fax no, mobile no, region, business type, no employees and so on. Try to indicate any unique fields (such as a job number) and also show how different tables relate to each other (very important). If you have any table definitions from existing systems then provide these as well indicating any changes that are required.

Operational Scenario
- Describe a set of scenarios that illustrate, from the user's perspective, what will be experienced when using the system the system under various situations. For example, this would describe how different users would use the system and the typical sequence of actions that each would take.

Schedule and Budget
- Describe what timescale you are working to, any critical deadlines, any management constraints (e.g. nobody available to discuss the project during August, awaiting approval to proceed, etc) and the budget you are working to etc.

Appendices
- Include other information here that may be useful in understanding your requirements. For example definitions of industry specific terms, acronyms, abbreviations.

You can see from this that defining obtaining the requirements definition is a very important part of any database design. The company cited makes their living from providing database solutions, and to save time and effort they require as much detail as possible from the client. In the example that we are using, there is no client as such because it is a hypothetical situation. Nevertheless we can make assumptions about the system that is required in order to describe the approach to design. If in future you are engaged on a database design project where there exists a client, then the approach described here, and the questions given above, should be a good starting point towards obtaining a requirements specification.

Thus it is seen that a requirements specification should define the full functionality of the system, which includes both the functional and non-functional components. After the requirements have been established the next phase of the project is to establish a plan of activity.

5.3.   Planning

The Internet is a very rich resource for locating these tools, and some will also be offered on a free trial period. The difficulty here is that before you can apply any of these tools, you need to learn how to use them. This takes time and it has to be evaluated against the available resources. In the early stages of project management it is a good idea to spend time thinking about the project, sketching a few ideas using a pencil and paper and trying to find out any potential difficulties. In modern project management perhaps the overriding factor is the cost of the project. A cost estimate establishes the base line of the project cost at different stages of the project.

Time is another very important aspect to project management. The general approach to managing time is to divide a project into a number of definable tasks.

Typically this division would start with the requirements specification and would identify the major activities such as for example, design, development, integration, test, production etc. Depending on their complexity, these could be further subdivided into self-contained tasks, for example, design user Interface, develop database software, develop prototype bard etc. For each one of these tasks it is important to identify the team or person responsible to deliver it. If the task is going to be performed by a team, then a team leader must be appointed to manage it. In any case, whether it is a team or a single person delivering the task, all the components that are involved need to be identified during the planning stage.

For most small scale, science and engineering projects Gantt charts are a convenient method of representing tasks, their duration and in some cases inter-task dependencies can also be included. Although it is possible to purchase project management software that can be used to produce Gantt charts, these can also be easily produced in a package such as Excel spreadsheet. The most important part of constructing the chart is to ensure that the tasks are suitably allocated in time, sequence and any dependency. This is the responsibility of the project manager and the team involved in the planning phase. Experts in the relevant disciplines would normally be consulted in order to give a candid estimate of time and resources that are needed in order to complete a task. The principal aims of a Gantt chart are as follows,

- Schedule the Tasks
- Assess Start Point for Each (Possibly Relative to Progress of Others)
- Assumes Some Sequence/Dependency Analysis Has Been Conducted
- Insert Milestones
- Key Review/Delivery/Test Points
- Evaluate the Result
- Staff Profile (is it Reasonable)
- Make Necessary Adjustments (Schedule, Resource Mix, etc.)

Example Gantt Chart

Assume that you are an analyst programmer and that you are assigned a project to design and build a database application in Microsoft Access. The initial design brief that you have obtained from the client is as follows:

You are required to design a computerised database system for a town library.

The system must enable the user to perform the following tasks:
- Store a catalogue registered users as well as books, CDs and DVDs (catalogue items) that are in the library.
- The system must be able to control and monitor transactions of items loaned to users.
- Allow registered users to log in. Administrators should have a separate login username and password.
- Allow all users to monitor loan duration on items and allow only the administrators to issue reminders when items are overdue for returns.
- Allow all users to search for a particular item by author or ID number
- The administrator must be able to add and delete items as well registered users and change their description. The standard user will not be able to do this.

Your design should be implemented in Microsoft Access database and you have six weeks to deliver a solution.

With this client brief I am able to sketch out a preliminary schedule of activity. My time resource is 6 weeks and my initial schedule is as given in Table 5.1. I drafted my initial time schedule based on my experience in the subject and my understanding of what is required. My reasoning in allocating the time resources as given in Table 5.1, is as follows.

I have no previous experience in database design projects but I have just completed a short course lasting entitled 'Database Fundamentals'. This means that I have an idea of how to proceed with design and I also have working knowledge of Microsoft Access database.

For these reasons I have identified 6 tasks and 5 milestones as shown in Table 5.1. I have also indicated the amount of time that I think each task will take.

Note that the Gantt chart may change as my work evolves, but even so it is a good idea to have an outline time allocation at the start of the project.

Table 5.1. Project Gantt chart

Tasks	Duration (Days)																													
	1	2	3	4	5	6	7	8	9	10	11	12	13	14	15	16	17	18	19	20	21	22	23	24	25	26	27	28	29	30
Problem definitions	█	█	█	█	█	█	█	█	█	█																				
Requirements investigation and analysis			█	█	█	█	█	█	█	█	█	█	█	█	█	█	█	█	█	█										
Possible solutions						█	█	█	█	█	█	█	█	█	█	█	█	█	█	█										
Design														█	█	█	█	█	█	█										
Implementation and testing																	█	█	█	█	█	█	█	█	█	█	█	█	█	█
Project documentation																					█	█	█	█	█	█	█	█	█	█
Milestones			1										2							3								4		5
M1 - Project definition																														
M2 - Requirements document complete																														
M3 - Complete final design																														
M4 - Complete implementation and Testing																														
M5 - Complete documentation																														

My Gantt chart assumes that I shall be working 5 days a week for 6 weeks, giving total project duration of 30 days. This is non negotiable and I have to complete within this timescale. I have allocated 10 days to the task of problem definition and information gathering. Note that after day 3, I have established the project definition. From this point I allocate 17 days to analysis. I believe that this is justified because I want to ensure that the client and I concur on what my solution will provide. Note also that within 3 days of starting the analysis I am also beginning to consider possible solutions. This is to help to ensure that I am not presuming a single solution at the outset, which may not be the best one. Within 2 weeks of starting I have completed my requirements document and this is indicated by milestone M2. I am now in the position to begin the design task. Within tree days from this point I am also beginning the implementation in Access. My implementations runs in parallel with design as I am considering the database structure and at the same time implementing it to see how it all fits together. By the end of week 4, I have completed my design and this is indicated by milestone M3 and I am focusing on completing the implementation. At the same time I am working on the documentation that will accompany my solution. By day 28 I have completed my implementation and testing and this is indicated as milestone M4. I have the last two days to complete the documentation and this is indicated by milestone M5.

Note that the above Gantt chart is just an example of how you can use it to plan your work. You may well decide to break the project into more tasks and milestones and to allocate different timescales. All this will depend on what you think has to be done and roughly how much time you need to complete it. Nevertheless, I hope that the above example will help you in your planning.

5.4. Chapter summary

In this chapter I cover the basics of project management. This is a very broad area of study and it would be difficult to cover all aspects even if these were done as an overview. For this reason I provide an approach that I consider well suited to management database projects. I consider steps such as project definition, planning and modelling as well as the requirements analysis, which is extremely important throughout a project lifecycle. I also include an example of a Gantt chart as a method of planning projects. It is a simplified example, which should be sufficient to start with.

Exercises
5.1. Discuss the responsibilities of a project manager.
5.2. Explain the various stages of project management.
5.3. Discuss the main features of requirements engineering.
5.4. What documentation should be provided as part of the requirement process?
5.5. What are the benefits of a requirement specification?
5.6. Distinguish using examples between user and systems requirements documents.
5.7. How do you differentiate between functional and non-functional requirements? Give examples of each of these.
5.8. Describe the typical contents of a requirements definition document. How would this document differ from a user as opposed to system perspectives?
5.9. What is a Gantt chart used for?
5.10.Why are milestones important in Gantt charts?
5.11.Do a plan including a Gantt Chart for the following projects:
   o Database to record transactions and stock in a small flower shop. Make assumptions as necessary. You have 4 weeks to develop it in MS Access.
   o Database for a local school to monitor pupils and their performance. No financial information, just pupils and associated data. You have 10 weeks to develop it in MS Access.
   o A database of an on-line e-commerce business selling kitchen appliances to the public. You may make any assumptions, but it should be a major project that you will complete in 6 months. You will need to do some preliminary research into the tools that you might need for this, including the database that you would use.

CHAPTER 6   DATABASE PROJECT CASE STUDY

6.1.   Introduction

This chapter will consider the steps that you need to take in order to design and implement a database solution for a client. The project chosen is a typical town library and you are required to perform the full project cycle from initial specification through to design and onto implementation and testing. At the end you are required to produce two reports; one for the user and another for technical personnel. A brief outline of this process is given in order to guide you and to perhaps use this example as a template for any future database work that you do.

6.2.   Case study

Assume that you are an analyst programmer and that you are assigned a project to design and build a database application in Microsoft Access. The initial design brief that you have obtained from the client is as follows:

> *You are required to design a computerised database system for a town library.*
>
> *The system must enable the user to perform the following tasks:*
> * *Store a catalogue registered users as well as books, CDs and DVDs (catalogue items) that are in the library.*
> * *Be able to control and monitor transactions of items loaned to users.*
> * *Allow registered users to log in. Administrators should have a separate login username and password.*
> * *Allow all users to monitor loan duration on items and allow only the administrators to issue reminders when items are overdue for returns.*
> * *Allow all users to search for a particular item by author or ID number.*
> * *The administrator must be able to add and delete registered users as well as loan items and change their description. The standard user will not be able to do this.*
>
> *Your design should be implemented in Microsoft Access database.*

To help you with your design and development work I have included guidelines below. These guidelines are designed to tell you how you should approach the problem, carry out the design and implementation and what evidence you must submit to support your work. As you experience in database design grows, so you will develop your own approach to design, but until then the following approach should serve as useful guidelines. Your approach to designing the database should include the following stages.
* **Stage 1** Problem identification
* **Stage 2** Possible solution
* **Stage 3** Design
* **Stage 4** Development and testing
* **Stage 5** Documentation

Stage 1

You can see from the above that before you begin your actual design you need to define the problem and to consider possible solutions. Both these stages need to have the appropriate analysis so that you can be sure that you have explored the available options towards a solution. In Chapter 4 I mentioned that your approach to designing the database should include the following steps.

- **Step 1:** Obtain requirements specification. This means that you have to identify the task in hand and obtain a clear problem definition. This takes time and you need to analyse the client brief and have further meetings with them in order to arrive at the problem specification. This is explained in the example to follow. Essentially this work involves stage 1 above.

Stage 2

After the requirements have been established you need to provide analysis of the possible solutions. This falls under the category of Stage 2 above, which is concerned with the possible solutions. Considering design steps recommended in Chapter 4 this will involve the following.

- **Step 2:** Draw system context. This is the original model of the system that is used as a starting point for design.
- **Step 3:** Identify the entities in from the specification and use these to decide on the tables that you need. Use the Nouns in the specification to help you to identify the entities.
- **Step 4:** Describe attributes of each entity, to avoid data redundancy do not include a field if it can be calculated from other fields. Designate a primary key for each table. Use the adjectives in the specification to help you to identify the attributes.
- **Step 5:** Describe the relationships between the entities and designate the foreign keys to reflect these relationships.
- **Step 6:** Normalise the tables.

Note that it is not necessary to formally write each of these steps during design and normally it is sufficient that you are satisfied that you have covered these in your design.

Stage 3

During this stage you provide details of the actual design of your solution to the problem. You are not implementing the solution; instead you are designing it and considering the design options. It is unlikely that you will alter your design significantly, but minor changes are to be expected at this stage. Once again you will need to provide some analysis to show that you have approached the solution in an informed manner.

Stage 4

During this stage you are committed to the design that you have made and you provide details of the actual implantation and testing of your solution. Should you find errors in design at this stage, you will modify your design to correct this. It is customary to come across situation where minor changes to design become necessary as you begin to implement the solution.

Stage 5

The final stage is to produce the documentation for your solution to the problem identified in stage 1. Documentation is extremely important and sufficient time needs to be devoted to providing the appropriate detail for the different users of the system. You need to document the work that you have done so that users know how to use the system. You should also document technical aspects that will help others to maintain as well modify the solution if necessary.

The example to follow is intended to give you an idea of how a typical design could proceed from the initial client brief and towards the solution. My approach to this is to give you a brief description of the general futures of each stage and then provide an example solution for this stage.

6.3.   Stage 1:   Problem identification

This should include problem definition, investigation and analysis. A brief description of these components is given next.

Problem definition

This is a description of the nature of the problem. In some database applications this is also called the Scope. Every project has an aim and in this case you are a systems analyst who is charged with delivering a database solution. Your client is very important since they will be paying for this development and will be using the end product. For this reason you will need to have regular meetings with the client so that you can establish their precise requirements. In order to define the problem you will have to meet with the client and for this meeting you will prepare a series of interview questions for them to answer.

The analyst needs to find out, in detail, what the end user wants from the system. The general approach is to arrange an interview with the end user. This is not a matter of the analyst having a general chat with their end user, rather it should be a detailed discussion where the end user can present their idea of the system that they desire and also try to answer the questions that the analyst has prepared. The analyst must plan this meeting and typically it will involve more than simply reading from a questionnaire. In other words the analyst should go into the interview with a series of well-prepared questions to ask. However, they should not be asked as a simple list. If this is all that is done, the interview is a waste of time; the end-user could simply have filled in a questionnaire. The analyst must identify the areas that could be critical in the implementation and so these questions must be prepared before the interview.

The whole point about an interview is that the questioning should be flexible. The analyst should have `starter' questions on each of the areas to which they want answers. They should also have prepared a series of follow up questions that can be used, which are dependent upon the answer to the initial question.

You have to bear in mind that the analyst is trained in database design and is aware of limitations and implications of any feature that the client desires. They can advise the client what the consequences are of implementing their desired functionality, whether the impact is in terms of cost, performance, capacity etc.

Typically the analyst will have a series of meetings with the client and the outcomes of each of these will be analysed so that the most accurate representation of the desired system can be obtained. See the requirements specification section covered in Chapter 5 of this text for examples of the information needed from the client.

Investigation and analysis of the problem.

In this section you consider the background information that is available for the system, which needs to be designed. As soon as it is possible to do so you should start thinking about possible solutions. For example, the analysts must consider that there are different people involved in this organisation. In the above example, I have identified for you that there are a number of users as well as the administrator. As an example, you may assume that the maximum number of registered users on the system is 1,000. At this stage the analyst may choose to gather information from these users in order to learn from these people about the desirable features of the solution that has to be provided. Using different methods of collection can do this. For example, a sample of users (how are they to be chosen?) could be sent a questionnaire. Typically for this section you will need to describe the following aspects.

- **Organisation**. A description of the organisation for which the design is required and where the problem is within it. This information must come from the client and it serves to identify the problem.
- **Present situation**. A description of how the problem is dealt with at the moment. Before you can provide a solution you must know how the system is being run at the moment. This gives you a perspective on the situation that can enable you to identify the impact of any solution that you propose.
- **Data**. A clear description of the data that is used in the area of the problem. Here you will need to consider the data that is needed to help you maintain a record of lending in a library. Note that the exact data that will form part of the solution is as yet not known because the problem has not been fully specified; however, it is necessary to be aware of all the data that may be required.
- **Data source**. A clear indication of where the data came from? How it is collected? Much of this information may not be known. The analyst may have to make and clearly state any assumptions at this stage.

As an example, for the case study we can therefore formulate the following definition, which is based on the analyst having performed the tasks outlined above.

Example: Problem definition

A small town library requires a computerised database system. The library stores a wide variety of books, CDs and DVDs that are available on loan. DVDs and CDs are available for one-week loan while books are available for four-week loan.

The library employs the Librarian, the Assistant Librarian, and the Library Assistant. The responsibilities of these staff members are outlined next.

The Librarian:
- Creating new member records and new item records.
- Updating or editing existing member records and existing items records.
- Creating, updating, and editing employee records.
- Managing item loans and returns.
- Charging for overdue items.
- Generally, responsible for running the library with full access to data.

The Assistant Librarian:
- Creating new or updating and editing existing item records.
- Recording item loans and returns.
- Generally, assisting the librarian with limited access to data.

The Library Assistant:
- Placing the items in their original places on the shelf and assisting members with general enquiries.
- No access to data.

Present situation

At present the system for lending out is paper based. Each registered user has a paper card, and this is updated with any materials that they borrow. This card is kept at the library at all times. Likewise the book, CD or Video that is taken out, has a paper card, which is updated with return date after it is taken out.

The computer system in the library was recently upgraded. It consists of four computers connected in a network and is configured as a workgroup. Each computer has Windows XP Professional installed and a copy of the Microsoft Office Professional edition. All users of the system have basic computer skills and can easily be trained to use a computerised database system

Data

Data recorded for each item include:
- Books: Library Reference, Title, Author, Publisher, ISBN, Shelf No., Land-out Date, Return Date.
- CDs: Library Reference, Title, Artist, Shelf No., Land-out Date, Return Date.
- DVDs: Library Reference, Title, Director, Shelf No., Land-out Date, Return Date.
- Data recorded for each member include: Member ID, Name, Address, and Telephone.
- Data recorded for each employee include: Employee ID, Name, Address, Telephone, and Job Title.

Data source

All information is stored in a cabinet containing the cards of registered users. At the same time each book or CD/DVD has a sleeve where the information that the lender needs to know is recorded. This includes the registration number of the lender, the sign out date and the return date. When a book is loaned out both the user card and the book/CD/DVD card are updated to reflect the transaction.

All user cards are kept in a single room and book/CD/DVDs cards are kept inside a book/CD. There is a list of all the books/CDs/DVDs in the inventory file and this is updated whenever a change in the inventory takes place.

6.4. Stage 2   Possible solutions

Having collected all the information regarding the problem in stage 1, different types of solution may present themselves for consideration and this is the next stage of development. In the client brief given earlier I have suggested that a Microsoft Access database solution is required. However, you will still need to consider how the database will be shared with users. It is likely that different solutions will be possible and you need to consider these.

These different types of solutions must be considered as they provide a pointer towards the solution to the problem. The different approaches should be discussed with the end-user and the responses should be noted. You may choose to have a meeting with the client in order to discuss the implication of any possible solution. Therefore, at this stage you are not committed to any solution, and you are simply investigating the solutions that are available in order to be in the position to select the best one. At the end of this stage you should be in the position to provide the full requirements specification for the system to be designed. A requirements specification for the project outlines the details of the solution that you will provide to the client. It is often used as a legal basis for a contract between the client and the database analyst/programmer.

The following is an example of the type of investigation and analysis that could be put forward in the case study example of a town library database solution.

Example: Investigation and analysis

Currently most of the administrative work and record keeping is paper based, which consumes resources and time, and also causes some difficulties in communication and information coordination. For example, it is difficult to keep track of member's interests or overdue items. A member wishing to borrow an item or to find if an item is available usually spends a lot of time looking for this item.

After reviewing the old paper based records and discussing with the librarian a list of operational rules has been made as follows:
- Anyone who lives in the town can become a member of the library.
- The librarian can approve a membership only.
- The librarian must be able to contact members by telephone and by mail.
- The librarian must be able to keep track of each member's interests, so when the new item come in the librarian alerts members whose interests match those items.
- A member can check out any number of items in a visit.
- The librarian must be able to identify whether an item is loaned out.
- All books that are loaned out are due back in two weeks time and CDs and DVDs in one week. The late fee is one pound per day late for each item.
- A member is not allowed to borrow additional items before returning overdue items and paying overdue charges.
- Each employee has a job title. The librarian and assistant librarian are paid annual salary and the library assistant is paid by the hour.
- Only the librarian is allowed to update and maintain member and employee records.
- The assistant librarian is allowed to update item records and the item loan records.
- The library assistant is allowed to view item records but not to add or edit these.

After analysis of operational rules and further interviews with the librarian and the potential users the list of specifications and requirements for the new database system has been made as follows.

The computerised system should support the following features:
- Allow members to access the database system using one of the three user computers where they can search for items that they wish to borrow.
- Allow members to reserve items if they are not available at the time.
- Allow members to search for items by item ID, authors, artists, actors, publisher and description.
- Allow potential members to submit their details for membership.
- Enable the librarian to issue reminders when items are nearly overdue for returns.
- The librarian should be able to add and delete item records, member records and employee records. Standard users should not be able to do that.
- The librarian should be able to keep track of member's interests, current borrowing and overdue.
- The librarian should be able to generate a list of all overdue items each day.
- The librarian should be able to record payments for overdue charges.
- The assistant librarian should be able to add or update item records, and record the item loans.

As an example of the reasoning behind the possible solutions we can consider the following.

The goal of this project is to develop a computerised application that will address the problem areas of the library system. A computerised system would be more communicative, collaborative and efficient than a paper based one. It would centralise the information and make it more available and accessible to all interested parties.

There are few possible solutions to achieve this. One of them could be to configure the client/server network and develop the database application using MySQL software package, and to locate this centrally on the server, which would make the database more secure but would introduce an extra cost for the hardware and the software licensing. Another solution is to keep the current Workgroup network configuration and develop the database application using MS Access software package and store it on the librarian's computer. In this case the database should be stored in a shared folder so it can be accessed from other workstations.

Taking into account the size of the library, the number of users, the specifications and rules the second solution satisfies all the users requirements with no extra cost. One of the requirements is to allow members to access the database from one of the computers dedicated to members. This can be achieved in two ways: creating user account with minimal privileges for each member and allowing a member to log on, or creating only three accounts one for each computer dedicated to members with minimal privileges and allowing only librarians to log on into the database with full privileges. The first option introduces quite a lot administration to maintain user accounts and the second option requires only three accounts (station1, station2 and station3) and that these computers are logged on and ready for use before opening of the business.

Considering the second option as the adopted solution where each computer must have a copy of MS Access installed and the location of the shared folder on the librarian computer, where the database file is stored, must be mapped to each computer allocated for use by registered members.

The above considerations only serve as an example of the general approach towards defining and adopting a solution to the design problem. Having arrived at the recommendation of an appropriate solution we can proceed to the design stage.

6.5.   Stage 3   Design

The design stage follows on from investigation and analysis and at this point you are as ready as you can be to begin designing the system. The approach to design should include the following components.

- Nature of the solution provides a description of the features that the solution will provide.
- Intended benefits are used to demonstrate how the solution will benefit the client.
- Limitations of the scope of the solution describe the boundaries of your solution. The time and resources that are available often determine these.

An example design for the case study is given next.

Example design: Nature of the solution

Based on the information about the library and its users, and the requirements a list of objectives has been made as follows:

1. To design a table structure and relationships between tables, that will enable users to:

- Maintain records of members and their interests.
- Maintain records of employees and their salaries.
- Maintain records of items and their authors, artists, actors, directors, publishers etc.
- Maintain records of item loans and returns.
- Maintain records of item bookings.
- Maintain records of payments of overdue charges

2. To design forms that will enable authorised users to:
- Open the other forms (menus).
- Input a new member details into the members table, or edit existing member details in the members' table.
- Input a new employee into the employee table, or edit existing employee details in the employees' table.
- Input a new item into the items table, or edit existing items in the items table.
- Input a new author, artist, actor, category into their tables.
- Input an item loan details into the borrowing table.
- Update an item loan details when an item is returned.
- Input an item booking details into the booking table.
- Input an enrolment details for the new membership into the members table.
- Input a payment details into the payment table,
    - i.   View current borrowing by member.
    - ii.   View overdue items by member.
    - iii. Search for the items by the item ID, author, title, artist, actor, director and description .

3. To design queries and reports that will enable authorised users to:
- List all items whose loan is close to expire.
- List all items currently on loan and the return dates and days left.
- List all items that are overdue and display charges.
- List all items that are currently booked.

4. To design the security system that will enable,

Librarian to:
- Have a full access to all tables, forms and queries.

Assistant Librarian to:
- Add records into items table, borrowing table and the return table, but no privileges to add or edit records in any other table or form.

Members to:
- Search for items and reserve items with no access to data.
- Submit details for the membership through the enrolment form.

At this point you document the actual design. An example design is given in the appendix for your consideration.

In relation to the library example, and the proposed solution the following is an example of the intended benefits and the limitation of the solution.

Example design: Intended benefits

The new computerised system will bring a significant improvement to the old paper-based system. Firstly it will reduce the space for keeping the data and secondly it will considerably speed up the process of collecting, storing and retrieving the data. The users will be able to search for items and their availability very quickly. The new system will also enable the Librarian to closely monitor each member's reading interests, current borrowings or to monitor loan duration and issue charges for items that are overdue. Generally the system will speed up the information search and processing.

Example design: Limits of the scope of the solution

A full description of the contents and data types stored in each of the files together with the approximation of their size is given in the appendix under sub section "Table structures". Based on the assumption that the library has got 1,000 members and it stores 20,000 items the total size of the complete database solution would be approximately 5.1MB. Also based on the assumption that the library will generate 50 borrowing sessions with 100 items borrowed each day and 100 item bookings each month and 100 item overdue charges each month the database will grow by approximately 1MB every year.

As mentioned earlier the library computer network consists of four computers configured as a workgroup. Each computer belongs to the entry-level hardware configuration system with the Pentium 4 processor and the minimum of 40 GB of secondary storage space. There is also a Laser Jet printer connected to the network with the ability to print larger printouts. Considering the hardware available and a MS Access application as tailoring software the current database design provides a good solution for the organisation of this size. The two major limitation of the solution are that the actual payments and the invoicing for the item overdue charges are handled externally and the employee salaries are managed externally.

Once again the above are just examples of the type of analysis that is required under each section. Having outlined the design we proceed with the stage concerned with implementation and testing. This is covered next.

6.6. Stage 4 Database development, testing and implementation.

- **Development** deals with the strategy towards implementing the solution. Here you will consider the types of development strategies that are available. You can choose a strategy such as evolutionary prototyping, throwaway prototyping, incremental development etc.
- **Implementation** and testing provide insight into how you build the system and where the testing is done. In large database developments where a number of analysts are engaged to develop different components of the solution, this stage would also involve the integration of these components and testing of the system.
- **Appropriateness of structure** and exploitation of available facilities considers how efficient the solution is in regard to the resources that are available. To establish this it is necessary to define specific testing strategies.

Design details and the testing plan for the example of a town library are provided in the appendix but the general idea behind testing is that, since you have designed the solution, you are the best person to design the tests for it. You will design these tests to see whether the solution is doing what you expect it to. In order to assure yourself that this is indeed the case you have to design a test sequence. As an example for your consideration a possible design of the solution is covered in the appendix. You can use this as a guide to see what level of detail is required in your design. Tests should be designed to satisfy the designer that the system is working according to the specifications. There are a large number of ways that tests can be organised and arranged, but the following is a good starting point for the database example.

Testing should be structured; this means that you should design a test with a title, an aim, a method or procedure and the expected outcomes. After the test is completed you should observe the outputs from the test and discuss what they tell you. An example, a test for data input in the library database case study is given next. This is only an example to show the general template for a test specification and more tests for the library database solution example are listed in the appendix.

Example: Test results

Test title: **Data Input**

Aim: To input the new member details into the Enrolment form and check if they show up on the NewMember sub form.

Expected outcome: The newly entered details should be displayed on the NewMember sub form on the Member form.

Method: Details for the new membership were entered and submitted through the Enrolment form (Figure 6.1). The Member table below (Figure 6.2) shows the state of the table before new details were entered through the Enrolment form.

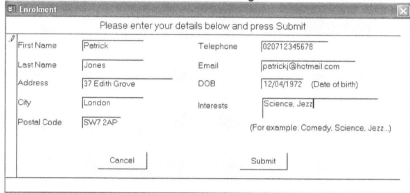

Figure 6.1

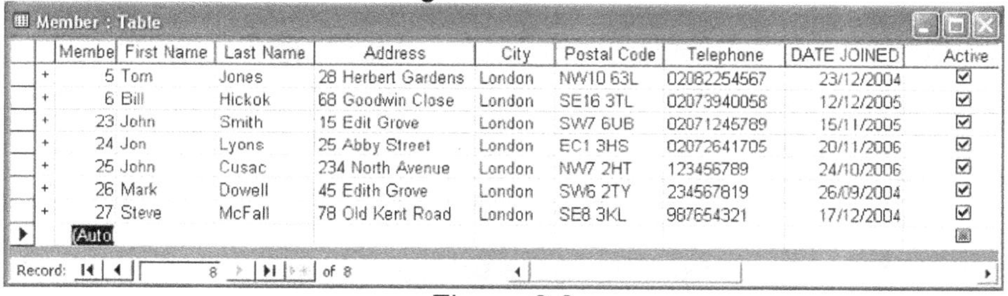

Figure 6.2

Results: The newly submitted details were picked up on the New Member sub form and displayed in the personal details section of the Member form (Figure 6.3). At this time the details are not updated (Date Joined missing and Interests not entered) and the membership is not active. The Member table below (Figure 6.4) shows the state of the table after new details were entered through the Enrolment form. The fields Date Joined and Active have not been set because the Librarian has not approved the membership.

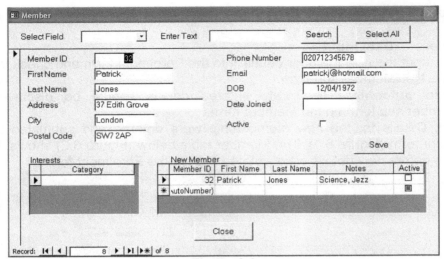

Figure 6.3

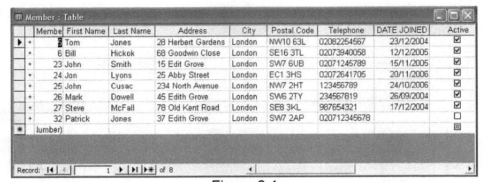

Figure 6.4

6.7. Stage 5 Database project documentation

The documentation that you provide to the client must include all the information that is needed to use and maintain the solution that you have provided. In general this will include the following documents,

- **Technical documentation:** This will be useful to developers and analysts who will look after the database solution and if necessary update it and modify it as time goes on. Documents provided in the appendix are an example of technical documentation.
- **User documentation:** This includes a description of how the user interacts with the solution and this includes troubleshooting and error codes as appropriate. I have not included in the appendix user documentation because it is only useful when software is available for the user, and this is not the case with my example. However it should be relatively easy for you to produce user documentation after you have implemented the software solution. User documentation is a guide for the person who is intending to use the system. Unlike a technical person, the user does not need to understand how the solution works but they do need to know how to work with it.
- **Project evaluation and concluding remarks:** Discussion of the degree of success in meeting the original objectives. Here you can also evaluate the user's response to the system. These will include the results of tests that will determine how good the system is at meeting the requirements outlined in the specification. Concluding remarks are usually focused on the aims and

objectives, and to what extent these have been satisfied. For example, this could include lists of those parts of the system that are satisfactorily completed, as well as a list of those areas that have not been successful.

- **Recommended further work:** It is common for project reports to consider what further work can be done to improve their solution. However well a system works there are always going to be extra things that could be done, rough edges that could be smoothed out, new hardware that could be used to give an improved finished product etc.

Example: Documentation

Example of technical documentation is given in the appendix. User documentation has not been included because it would only be relevant if the software were made available.

6.8. Chapter summary

This chapter provides an example of how a design of a database solution can be approached. This is done through a case study of a typical town library. This example was selected because many readers will be familiar with the workings of a typical library. The problem is hypothetical and I have used assumptions in order to provide guidelines along which design should proceed. I have provided example solutions to the various stages of design while the technical documentation is provided in the appendix.

Exercises

6.1 Provide a design solution for the following projects: (you provided a plan for these in the exercises from Chapter 5)

- Database to record transactions and stock in a small flower shop. Make assumptions as necessary. You have 4 weeks to develop it in MS Access.
- Database for a local school to monitor pupils and their performance. No financial information, just pupils and associated data. You have 4 weeks to develop it in MS Access.
- A database of an on-line e-commerce business selling kitchen appliances to the public. You may make any assumptions, but it should be a major project that you will complete in 6 months. You will need to do some preliminary research into the tools that you might need for this, including the database that you would use.

References

All websites listed in this section were accessed during the period 01/09/2008-21/10/2008

Chapter 1

[1] Colin Ritchie, Relational Database Principles, Thomson 2005

[2] Brady/Monk, Problem solving Cases in Microsoft Access and Excel, Thomson Course Technology, 2004.

[3] Rob/Coronel , Database Systems: Design, Implementation and Management, Sixth Edition, Thomson Course Technology, 2004.

[4] G. Bezanov, Embedded programming for the 8051, an overview publication series, MIG Consulting Ltd, London, 2008.

[5] http://en.wikipedia.org/wiki/Sql

[6] http://www.ansi.org/about_ansi/introduction/introduction.aspx?menuid=1

[7] http://www.databasedev.co.uk/multi-user-applications.html

[8] http://msdn.microsoft.com/en-us/library/aa141385(office.10).aspx

[9] http://www.bettscomputers.com/distributeddatabase.htm

[10] http://www.bl.uk/collections/britishnewspapers1800to1900.html

[11] http://www.statistics.gov.uk/cci/nugget.asp?ID=19

[12] http://en.wikipedia.org/wiki/Database#Storage_and_physical_database_design

Chapter 2

[13] http://en.wikipedia.org/wiki/Database_model

[14] http://www.bestpricecomputers.co.uk/glossary/database-management-systems.htm

[15] http://en.wikipedia.org/wiki/Entity-relationship_model]

Chapter 3

[16] Microsoft access help

[17] Teresa Hennig, Rob Cooper, Geoffrey L. Griffith , Armen Stein , Access 2007 VBA Programmer's Reference, Wrox (May 14, 2007)

Chapter 4

[18] http://databases.about.com/od/specificproducts/a/normalization.htm

[19] http://www.tutorialized.com/view/tutorial/Database-design-tutorial/22154

Chapter 5

[20] Dennis D.L., Dennis L.B., Management Science, West Publishing Company, 1991

[21] http://www.businessballs.com/project.htm

[22] www.ieee.org

[23] http://www.aldex.co.uk/reqspec.html

[24] Robert Japenga, Software requirements Specification, How to write a software requirements specification

http://eent3.sbu.ac.uk/units/softwareengineering/speed/How%20to%20write%20a%20softw are%20requirements%20specification.htm

[25] Somerville, Ian, Software Engineering, Fourth Edition, Addison-Wesley Publishing Company, Wokingham, England, 1992

[26] http://en.wikipedia.org/wiki/Metrics

Chapter 6

[27] http://www.aldex.co.uk/reqspec.html

[28] Borislav Benak, Database fundamentals: Library Database technical documentation, 2007, London Southbank University assignment.

Appendix A – LIBRARY DATABASE

A.1 TECHNICAL DOCUMENTATION

Introduction

This technical report has been produced by Mr. Borislav Benak [28] in accordance with the specifications given in the example of a small town library in Chapter 6 of this text. Mr Benak also produced a user report as well as the database software, but these have not been included within this appendix. The aim of the appendix is to give you an idea of the contents of a typical technical report that accompanies a database design. It also shows the level of detail that needs to be included.

A.1.1 Background

This database solution is developed for a small town library. The library stores books, DVDs and CDs that are available on loan. It is assumed that the library will store approximately 20,000 items and it will have approximately 1,000 active members. The existing system in the library is paper based so the new computerised solution was developed from scratch.

DATABASE SYSTEM

The solution was developed using the MS Access software application with the support for VB programming. All data collected is stored in tables that hold related records. Data is input into the tables through user screens or forms that are specifically designed for that purpose. Each form is linked to one or more tables. The queries and reports are designed to retrieve and manipulate data or to print it out. The necessary hardware to run this solution will include two or more computer workstations running Windows XP operating system connected into the local area network and configured as Microsoft Workgroup.

RECOMMENDED HARDWARE AND SOFTWARE
Hardware
Two or more PC workstations with the following configuration:
- Pentium 4 class CPU or higher
- 512 MB RAM
- 20GB or more HDD space
- LAN card or controller

All workstations should be connected into local area network and configured as Microsoft Workgroup.

Software
Each workstation should have the following software installed:
- MS Windows XP Professional Operating System
- MS Office suit including Access database application

The Microsoft file and print sharing should be enabled and the folder where the database will be stored should be shared.

A.1.2 DATABASE MODEL

The database diagram (Figure A 1) illustrates the physical design of all tables in the library database. Database optimisation was attempted by implementing a level of data normalisation to eliminate data redundancy. Primary and foreign keys are used to create relationships between tables.

RELATIONSHIPS

Member ➜ Interests ⬅ Category ➜ Item
- The Member-Interests relationship is One-to-Many. A Member can have many interests.
- The Category-Interests relationship is One-to-Many. A category can generate many interests.
- The Category-Item relationship is One-to-Many. Many items can belong to one category.
- The Interests table joins the Member table with the Category table and handles multiple interests for one member.

Member ➜ Borrowing ➜ Borrow_Line ⬅ Item
- The Member-Borrowing relationship is One-to-Many. A Member can generate many borrowing sessions.
- The Borrowing-Borrow_Line relationship is One-to-Many. A borrowing session can hold many borrowing lines (a member can borrow many items in one session).
- The Item-Borrow_Line relationship is One-to-Many. An item can enter many borrowing lines (an item can be borrowed many times).
- The Borrow_Line table joins the Item table with the Borrowing table and handles multiple items in one borrowing session.

Member ➜ Booking ⬅ Item
- The Member-Booking relationship is One-to-Many. A member can make many bookings.
- The Item-Booking relationship is One-to-Many. An item can be booked many times.

Item ➜ Author_Lines ⬅ Author
- The Item-Author_Lines relationship is One-to-Many and the Author-Author_Lines relationship is One-to-Many. An item (book) can have many authors and an author can have many items. The Author_Lines table joins the Item table with the Author table and handles multiple entries.

Item ➜ Actor_Lines ⬅ Actor
- The Item-Actor_Lines relationship is One-to-Many and the Actor-Actor_Lines relationship is One-to-Many. An item (DVD) can have many actors and an actor can have many items (DVD). The Actor_Lines table joins the Item table with the Actor table and handles multiple entries.

Item ➜ Artist_Lines ⬅ Artist
- The Item-Artist_Lines relationship is One-to-Many and the Artist-Artist_Lines relationship is One-to-Many. An item (CD) can have many artists and an artist can have many items. The Artist_Lines table joins the Item table with the Artist table and handles multiple entries.

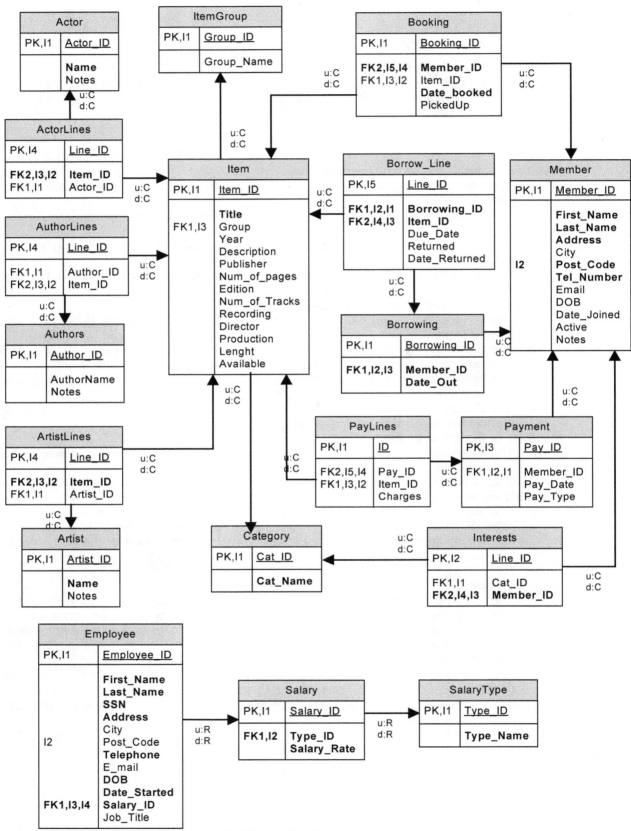

Figure A 1 Model for the database

96

Member ➔ Payment ➔ PayLines ⬅ Item

- The Member-Payment relationship is One-to-Many. A Member can generate many payment sessions.
- The Payment-PayLines relationship is One-to-Many. A payment session can hold many pay lines (a member can pay for many charges in one session).
- The Item-PayLines relationship is One-to-Many. An item can enter many pay lines (an item can generate many overdue charges).
- The PayLines table joins the Item table with the Payment table and handles multiple charges in one payment session.

Salary_Type ➔ Salary_Rate ➔ Employee

- The Salary_Type-Salary_Rate relationship is One-to-Many. One salary type can have many salary rates.
- The Salary_Rate-Employee relationship is One-to-Many. One salary rate can belong to many employees.

TABLE STRUCTURES
Member
The Member table shown in Table A 1, is designed to store all the necessary details about library members. The table will store approximately one thousand records.

In the Table A 1, the attribute Active shows if the membership has been activated. If the value is "Yes" than the Librarian has approved the membership and if is No the details are recently been submitted by a potential member and are waiting for approval.

Table A1 Member table with fields

KEY	FIELD	DATA TYPE	SIZE	REQUIRED
PK	Member_ID	AutoNumber	Long integer	Yes
	First_Name	Text	20 char	Yes
	Last_Name	Text	20 char	Yes
	Address	Text	25 char	Yes
	City	Text	15 char	No
	Post_Code	Text	10 char	Yes
	Tel_Number	Text	12 char	Yes
	Email	Text	20 char	No
	DOB	Time/Date	Short date	No
	Date_Joined	Time/Date	Short date	Yes
	Active	Yes/No	Boolean	No
	Notes	Text	50 char	No

Item
The Item table (A2) stores all the necessary details about library items. The items can be books, CDs and DVDs. This structure will introduce some Null fields in the table, for example if a book item is stored in the table the actor, artist, director, length, production and number of tracks will be empty, but it simplifies the table relations design. It is assumed that this table will hold approximately 20,000 records. The attribute Group represents the item group. Only three groups currently exist (Books, DVDs, and CDs) but a new group can be added. The attribute Available shows if an item is currently available for loan. This attribute is automatically set To Yes every time is borrowed and to No when is returned.

Table A 2 Item table

KEY	FIELD	DATA TYPE	SIZE	REQUIRED
PK	Item_ID	AutoNumber	Long integer	Yes
	Title	Text	25 char	No
FK	Group	Number	Long integer	Yes
FK	CategoryID	Number	Long integer	Yes
	Year	Text	5 char	No
	Description	Text	50 char	No
	Publisher	Text	20 char	No
	NumofPages	Text	5 char	No
	Edition	Text	2 char	No
	NumofTracks	Text	2 char	No
	Recording	Text	20 char	No
	Director	Text	20 char	No
	Production	Text	20 char	No
	Length	Text	6 char	No
	Available	Yes/No	Boolean	Yes

Group

The Group table (A3) stores the list of item groups. At present there are only three groups of items, books, CDs and DVDs. The new group can be easily added for the future expansion. The groups can be very useful for separating items in queries and input/output forms.

Table A 3 Group table

KEY	FIELD	DATA TYPE	SIZE	REQUIRED
PK	Group_ID	AutoNumber	Long integer	Yes
	Group_Name	Text	10 char	Yes

Category

The Category table (A4) stores the list of item categories such as fiction, drama, jazz or science. These categories will be used to identify which category each item belongs to or to specify each member's interests.

Table A 4 Category table

KEY	FIELD	DATA TYPE	SIZE	REQUIRED
PK	Cat_ID	AutoNumber	Long integer	Yes
	Cat_Name	Text	15 char	Yes

Interests

The Interests table (A5) presents the link between the Member table and the Category table. It stores the Member_ID and the Category_ID. The table is used to handle multiple category interests for each library member. It is assumed that this table will store approximately 3,000 records.

Table A 5 Interests table

KEY	FIELD	DATA TYPE	SIZE	REQUIRED
PK	Line_ID	AutoNumber	Long integer	Yes
FK	Cat_ID	Number	Long integer	Yes
FK	Member_ID	Number	Long integer	Yes

Author

The Author table (A6) holds the list of authors of all the books stored in the library. New authors can be added to the table without having to add new item into the Item table. It is assumed that this table will store approximately 2,000 records.

Table A 6 Author table

KEY	FIELD	DATA TYPE	SIZE	REQUIRED
PK	Author_ID	AutoNumber	Long integer	Yes
	AuthorName	Text	20 char	Yes
	Notes	Text	50 char	No

AuthorLines

The AuthorLines table (A7) presents the link between the Item table and the Author table. It stores the Item_ID and the Author_ID. The table is used to handle multiple authors for the book items. It is assumed that this table will hold approximately 20,000 records.

Table A 7 AuthorLines table

EY	FIELD	DATA TYPE	SIZE	REQUIRED
PK	Line_ID	AutoNumber	Long integer	Yes
FK	Item_ID	Number	Long integer	Yes
FK	Author_ID	Number	Long integer	Yes

Actor

The Actor table (A8) holds the list of actors of all the DVDs stored in the library. New actors can be added to the table without having to add new item into the Item table. It is assumed that this table will store approximately 2,000 records.

Table A 8 Actor table

KEY	FIELD	DATA TYPE	SIZE	REQUIRED
PK	Actor_ID	AutoNumber	Long integer	Yes
	ActorName	Text	20 char	Yes
	Notes	Text	50 char	No

ActorLines

The ActorLines table (A9) presents the link between the Item table and the Actor table. It stores the Item_ID and the Actor_ID. The table is used to handle multiple actors for each DVD item. It is assumed that this table will store approximately 25,000 records.

Table A 8 Actor lines table

KEY	FIELD	DATA TYPE	SIZE	REQUIRED
PK	Line_ID	AutoNumber	Long integer	Yes
FK	Item_ID	Number	Long integer	Yes
FK	Actor_ID	Number	Long integer	Yes

Artist

The Artist table (A 10) holds the list of artists of all the CDs stored in the library. New artists can be added to the table without having to add a new item into the Item table. It is assumed that this table will store approximately 3,000 records.

Table A 10 Artist table

KEY	FIELD	DATA TYPE	SIZE	REQUIRED
PK	Artist_ID	AutoNumber	Long integer	Yes
	ArtistName	Text	20 char	Yes
	Notes	Text	50 char	No

ArtistLines

The ArtistLines table (A 11) presents the link between the Item table and the Artist table. It stores the Item_ID and the Artist_ID. The table is used to handle multiple artists for the CD item. It is assumed that this table will store approximately 23,000 records.

Table A 11 Artist lines table

KEY	FIELD	DATA TYPE	SIZE	REQUIRED
PK	Line_ID	AutoNumber	Long integer	Yes
FK	Item_ID	Number	Long integer	Yes
FK	Artist_ID	Number	Long integer	Yes

Booking

The Booking table (A12) is used to store the item booking information. A member can book an item if one is not available at the time. The booking session is saved in this table. It is assumed that this table will grow by 100 records every month.

Table A 12 Booking table

KEY	FIELD	DATA TYPE	SIZE	REQUIRED
PK	Booking_ID	AutoNumber	Long integer	Yes
FK	Member_ID	Number	Long integer	Yes
FK	Item_ID	Number	Long integer	Yes
	Date_booked	Time/Date	Short date	Yes
	PickedUp	Yes/No	Boolean	No

The attribute PickedUp is used to control which items are currently booked. Once the item is picked up by a member who booked it this attribute is automatically set to Yes and the item is removed from the currently booked items list, which is generated by the Booking query.

Borrowing

The Borrowing table (A13) is used to record and save members borrowing sessions. A member can borrow many items in one session. It is assumed that this table will grow by 1500 records every month.

Table A 13 borrowing table

KEY	FIELD	DATA TYPE	SIZE	REQUIRED
PK	Borrowing_ID	AutoNumber	Long integer	Yes
FK	Member_ID	Number	Long integer	Yes
	Date_Out	Time/Date	Short date	Yes

BorrowLines

The table (A 14) is designed to link the Borrowing table with the Item table and to handle multiple items in one borrowing session. It is assumed that this table will grow by 3,000 records every month.

The attribute Due_Date represents the date that an item should be returned. Books are available for 14 days loan and DVDs and CDs for 7 days. The Date_Returned attribute represents the date when an item was actually returned. The attribute Returned is used in queries to show items that are currently on loan or items that are currently overdue. The attribute is automatically set to Yes when an item is returned.

Table A 14 Borrowing lines table

KEY	FIELD	DATA TYPE	SIZE	REQUIRED
PK	Line_ID	AutoNumber	Long integer	Yes
FK	Borrowing_ID	Number	Long integer	Yes
FK	Item_ID	Number	Long integer	Yes
	Due_Date	Time/Date	Short date	Yes
	Date_Returned	Time/Date	Short date	No
	Returned	Yes/No	Boolean	No

Payment

The Payment table (A15) is designed to store a member's payment details for item overdue charges. All items have a limited loan time. After that time has expired an overdue charges are introduced to the member that borrowed those items. It is assumed that this table will grow by 50 records every month.

Table A 15 Payment table

TABLE	KEY	FIELD	DATA TYPE	SIZE	REQUIRED
PAYMENT	PK	Pay_ID	AutoNumber	Long integer	Yes
	FK	Member_ID	Number	Long integer	Yes
		Pay_Date	Time/Date	Short date	Yes
		Pay_Type	Text	15 char	No

PayLines

The PayLines table (A 16) is designed to link the Payment table with the Item table and to handle multiple item charges in one payment session. It is assumed that this table will grow by 100 records every month. The attribute Charges shows a charge for every single item that was overdue.

Table A 16 Pay lines table

KEY	FIELD	DATA TYPE	SIZE	REQUIRED
PK	Line_ID	AutoNumber	Long integer	Yes
FK	Pay_ID	Number	Long integer	Yes
FK	Item_ID	Number	Long integer	Yes
	Charges	Currency	Long integer	Yes

Employee

The Employee table (A 17) is designed to store all the necessary details about library employees. The library has got three employees at present, so the table will store three records.

Table A 17 Employee table

KEY	FIELD	DATA TYPE	SIZE	REQUIRED
PK	Employee_ID	AutoNumber	Long integer	Yes
	First_Name	Text	20 char	Yes
	Last_Name	Text	20 char	Yes
	Address	Text	25 char	Yes
	City	Text	15 char	No
	Post_Code	Text	10 char	Yes
	SSN	Text	12 char	Yes
	Tel_Number	Text	12 char	Yes
	Email	Text	20 char	No
	DOB	Time/Date	Short date	No
	Date_Started	Time/Date	Short date	Yes
FK	Salary_ID	Number	Long integer	Yes

Salary

The Salary table (A 18) stores the details about employee's salary such as salary type and rate. The table will hold three records only.

Table A 18 Employee table

KEY	FIELD	DATA TYPE	SIZE	REQUIRED
PK	Salary_ID	AutoNumber	Long integer	Yes
FK	Type_ID	Number	Long integer	Yes
	Salary_Rate	Currency	Long integer	Yes

The Salary_Rate attribute stores a salary rate for a salary type. For example type Annual ➔ £25,000.

SalaryType

The SalaryType table (A 19) holds the list of different salary types such as annual salary, monthly salary and hourly salary. A new type can be added without adding a new employee. It is assumed that this table will store no more than four records.

Table A 19 salary type table

KEY	FIELD	DATA TYPE	SIZE	REQUIRED
PK	Type_ID	AutoNumber	Long integer	Yes
FK	Type_Name	Text	15 char	Yes

QUERIES

Booking

The Booking query (Figure A 2) lists all the items that are currently booked by members. When an item is returned the PickedUp attribute in the Booking table is set to "Yes" and the item is removed from this query.

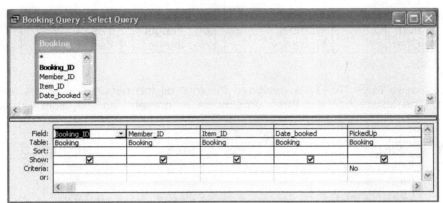

Figure A 2 Booking query generated in MSAccess

Record source: Table Booking.
SQL code:
```
SELECT Booking.Booking_ID, Booking.Member_ID,
Booking.Item_ID, Booking.Date_booked,        Booking.PickedUp
FROM    Booking
WHERE (((Booking.PickedUp)=No));
```

NewMember

The newMember query (Figure A 3) lists all users who submitted their details for the membership through the Enrolment form. When the membership has been approved by the Librarian the attribute Active in the Member table is set to "Yes" and the new member details are removed from this query.

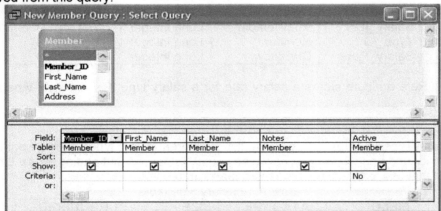

Figure A 3 Details of member query

Record source: Table Member.
SQL code:
```
SELECT Member.Member_ID, Member.First_Name,
Member.Last_Name, Member.Notes, Member.Active
FROM Member
WHERE (((Member.Active)=No));
```

102

LoanExpireNotification

This query (Figure A 4) is designed to list all items whose loan expires in less than three days. The query is used to generate a report, which is used by the Librarian to notify all members whose loan is about to expire. The Due_Date is the attribute in the Borrow_Line table, which represents the date that an item should be returned. Remaining days of the loan are calculated by subtracting the current date from the Due_Date.

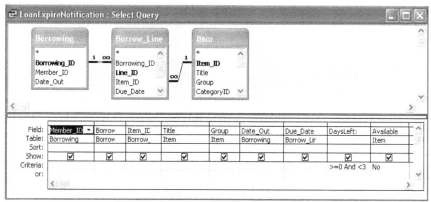

Figure A 4 Details of member query

Record source: Tables Borrowing, Borrow_Line and Item.
SQL code:
```
SELECT Borrowing.Member_ID, Borrowing.Borrowing_ID,
Borrow_Line.Item_ID, Item.Title, Item.Group,
Borrowing.Date_Out, Borrow_Line.Due_Date, [Due_Date]-Date()
AS DaysLeft, Item.Available
FROM Item INNER JOIN (Borrowing INNER JOIN Borrow_Line ON
Borrowing.Borrowing_ID=Borrow_Line.Borrowing_ID) ON
Item.Item_ID=Borrow_Line.Item_ID
WHERE ((([Due_Date]-Date())>=0 And ([Due_Date]-Date())<3)
AND ((Item.Available)=No));
```

CurrentBorrowing

The CurrentBorrowing query (Figure A 5) is designed to list all the items that are currently borrowed and by whom. It is linked to the CurrentBorrowing sub form on the BorrowReturn, the listed records are filtered by the members ID. Also the CurrentBorrowing report is generated from this query to provide the list for printing. The attribute Returned in the Borrow_Line table shows if an item has been returned. When the item has been returned this attribute is set to "Yes" and the item is removed from this query.

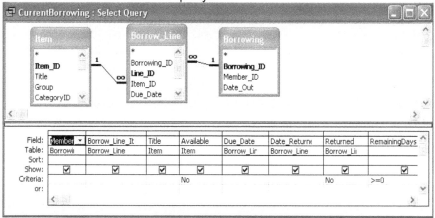

Figure A 5 Details of current borrowing query

Record source: Tables Item, Borrow_Line and Borrowing.
SQL code:

```
SELECT Borrowing.Member_ID, Borrow_Line.Borrowing_ID,
Borrow_Line.Item_ID AS Borrow_Line_Item_ID, Item.Title,
Item.Group, Item.Available, Borrowing.Date_Out,
Borrow_Line.Due_Date, Borrow_Line.Date_Returned,
Borrow_Line.Returned, [Due_Date]-Date() AS RemainingDays
FROM Item INNER JOIN (Borrowing INNER JOIN Borrow_Line ON
Borrowing.Borrowing_ID=Borrow_Line.Borrowing_ID) ON
Item.Item_ID=Borrow_Line.Item_ID
WHERE (((Item.Available)=No) AND ((Borrow_Line.Returned)=No)
AND (([Due_Date]-Date())>=0));
```

OverduebyMember

The OverduebyMember query (Figure A 6) is designed to list all the items that are overdue and by whom they were borrowed. The query is linked to the Overdue sub form on the BorrowReturn where the listed records are filtered by the members ID. The overdue items list is generated by subtracting the current date from the Due_Date and setting the criteria to display all items where remaining loan days are less than zero. Charges are calculated by multiplying the remaining days (overdue days) with a standard overdue charge per item.

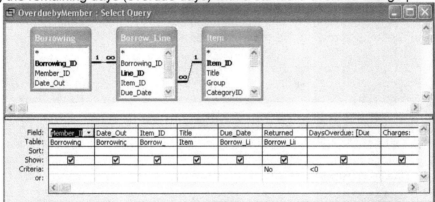

Figure A 6 Details of overdue payment query

Record source: Tables Borrowing, Borrow_Line and Item.
SQL code:

```
SELECT Borrowing.Member_ID, Borrowing.Borrowing_ID,
Borrowing.Date_Out, Borrow_Line.Item_ID, Item.Title,
Item.Group, Borrow_Line.Due_Date, Borrow_Line.Returned,
Borrow_Line.Date_Returned, [Due_Date]-Date() AS DaysOverdue,
[DaysOverdue]*(-1) AS Charges
FROM Item INNER JOIN (Borrowing INNER JOIN Borrow_Line ON
Borrowing.Borrowing_ID=Borrow_Line.Borrowing_ID) ON
Item.Item_ID=Borrow_Line.Item_ID
WHERE (((Borrow_Line.Returned)=No) AND (([Due_Date]-
Date())<0));
```

A.1.3 MENU SYSTEM

The Figure A 7 below shows the Menu System diagram.

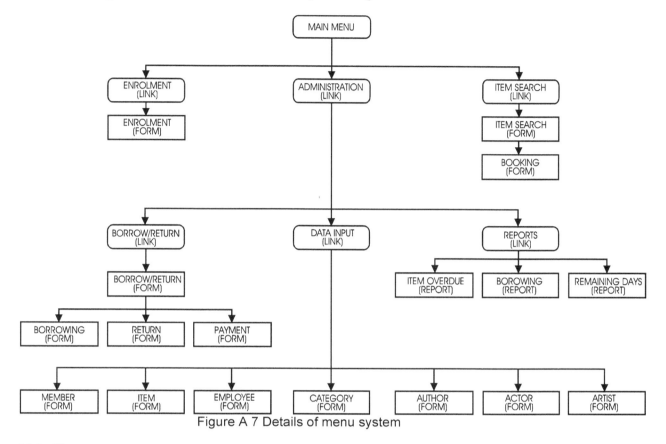

Figure A 7 Details of menu system

Main Menu

The Main Menu (Figure A 8) provides links to the Enrolment form, Item Search form and Administration Menu.

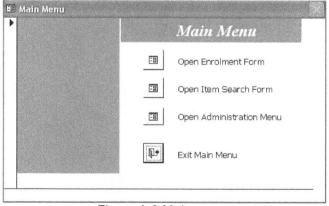

Figure A 8 Main menu

Administration Menu

The Administration Menu (Figure A 9) provides links to the Borrow/Return form, Data Input Menu and Reports Menu.

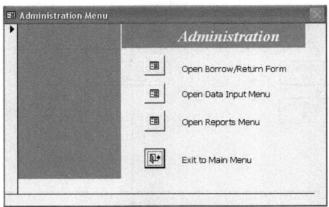

Figure A 9 Administration menu

Reports Menu

The Reports Menu (Figure A 10) provides links to the following reports: Booking, Current Borrowing, Item Overdue and Remaining Days.

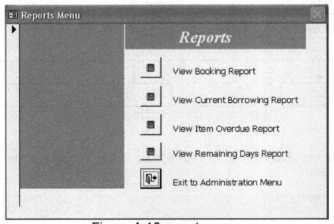

Figure A 10 reports menu

Data Input Menu

The Data Input Menu (Figure A 11) provides links to the following screens: Members, Items, Employees, Actors, Artists, Authors and Categories.

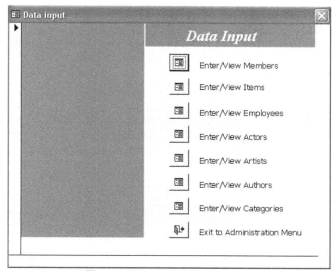

Figure A 11 data input menu

All buttons and object links in this menu system are created using the MS Access wizards and the codes generated for each button are very similar. For example:

```
Private Sub cmdMember_Click()
On Error GoTo Err_cmdMember_Click

    Dim stDocName As String
    Dim stLinkCriteria As String

    stDocName = "Member"
    DoCmd.OpenForm stDocName, , , stLinkCriteria
    DoCmd.Close acForm, "Data Input"
Exit_cmdMember_Click:
    Exit Sub

Err_cmdMember_Click:
    MsgBox Err.Description
    Resume Exit_cmdMember_Click

    End Sub
```

The only things that change for all buttons are the name of the subroutine and name of the object to be opened.

FORMS

All forms or user screens were developed by using the MS Access form wizard. The wizard generated necessary code that supports standard MS Access form features such as command buttons, opening forms, closing forms, form synchronisation, etc. Some additional code was written in VB to support additional features such as item search, input atomisation, input validation, etc and that code will be listed in this section.

Modules

This section stores all global subroutines or functions that are used in this database. Currently there are two modules whose code is listed below. This function checks if a parent form is loaded, and it is used to prevent some sub forms to be loaded if their parent form is not loaded.

```
Function IsLoaded(ByVal strFormName As String) As Boolean
 ' Returns True if the specified form is open in Form view
or Datasheet view.
    Dim oAccessObject As AccessObject

    Set oAccessObject = CurrentProject.AllForms(strFormName)
    If oAccessObject.IsLoaded Then
        If oAccessObject.CurrentView <> acCurViewDesign Then
            IsLoaded = True
        End If
    End If
End Function
```

Enrolment

The Enrolment form (Figure A 12) is used as an input screen where users who wish to become library members can submit their details. The form is configured as the entry form. The details entered through this form are saved in the Member table.

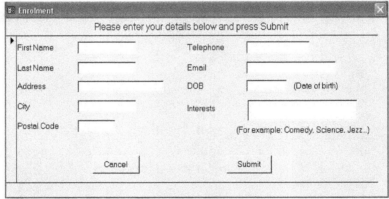

Figure A 12 Enrolment form

Member

The Member form (Figure A 13) is used to enter new members or to view existing member details. The search for a member details can be performed by selecting a search field such as ID, Name, Address, etc, entering the search text and pressing the search button. Select All button selects all members in the Member table. The form contains two sub forms, the Interest sub form and the New Member sub form.

Figure A 13 Details of member form

Record source: Member table.

The code below is attached to the OnClick event of the Select All button. It selects all members in the Member table.

```
Private Sub cmdSelectAll_Click()


    Dim LSQL  As String
    Dim SearchCriteria As String

    'Clears the search criteria
    SearchCriteria = ""

    'Selects all members from the table Member
    LSQL = "select * from Member"
    Form_Member.RecordSource = LSQL
    Form_Member.Caption = "Members (All members)"
    MsgBox "All members are now selected."


End Sub
```

This code is attached to the OnOpen event of the Member form and it is used to clear the search criteria, combobox and textbox.

```
Private Sub Form_Open(Cancel As Integer)
    SearchCriteria = ""
    cboSearchField = ""
    txtSearchString = ""


End Sub
```

The code below is attached to the OnClick event of the Search button and it is used to check that the combo box and the textbox are not empty, to build the search criteria based on the selection from the combo box and the text string entered into the textbox and select all members from the Member table based on the search criteria.

```
Private Sub cmdSearch_Click()
    'Checks that combo box and text box are not empty
    If Len(cboSearchField) = 0 Or IsNull(cboSearchField) =
True Then
```

109

```
        MsgBox "You must select a field to search"

    ElseIf Len(txtSearchString) = 0 Or
IsNull(txtSearchString) = True Then
        MsgBox "You must enter a search text"

    Else

        'Builds the search criteria
        SearchCriteria = cboSearchField.Value & " LIKE '*" &
txtSearchString & "*'"

        Form_Member.RecordSource = "select * from Member
where " & SearchCriteria

        MsgBox "Results have been selected"
        'Clears search criteria,combo box and text box
before exiting
        SearchCriteria = ""
        cboSearchField = ""
        txtSearchString = ""
    End If

End Sub
```

Interests sub form
The Interests sub form displays categories that a selected member is interested in.
Record source: Interests table.

The code below displays the massage if during the data input the entered category is not on the list and than enables a user to add the new category to the list by double clicking on the Interests sub form.

```
Private Sub CategoryID_NotInList(NewData As String, Response
As Integer)
    MsgBox "Double-click this field to add an entry to the
list."
    Response = acDataErrContinue
End Sub


Private Sub CategoryID_DblClick(Cancel As Integer)
On Error GoTo Err_CategoryID_DblClick
    Dim lngCategoryID As Long

    If IsNull(Me![CategoryID]) Then
        Me![CategoryID].Text = ""
    Else
        lngCategoryID = Me![CategoryID]
        Me![CategoryID] = Null
    End If
    DoCmd.OpenForm "Category", , , , , acDialog, "GotoNew"
    Me![CategoryID].Requery
    If lngCategoryID <> 0 Then Me![CategoryID] =
lngCategoryID
```

```
Exit_CategoryID_DblClick:
    Exit Sub


Err_CategoryID_DblClick:
    MsgBox Err.Description
    Resume Exit_CategoryID_DblClick
End Sub
```

New Member sub form

The New Member sub form displays the details for the membership that were submitted through the Enrolment form.

Record source: New Member Query.

The code below ensures that the New Member sub form cannot be opened independently. It can be viewed through the Member form only. The code is attached to the OnOpen event of the New Member sub form.

```
Private Sub Form_Open(Cancel As Integer)
Dim strMsg As String
Dim strTitle As String
Dim intStyle As Integer
Dim strFName As String
Dim strCForm As String

    strFName = "Member"
    strCForm = Me.Form.Name
    'Check if the parent form is loaded
    If IsLoaded(strFName) Then

Exit Sub

    Else
        strMsg = "You cannot open" & " " & strCForm & " " &
"as a standalone form." & vbCrLf & _
        "It can be viewed from the" & " " & strFName & "
form"

        intStyle = vbOKOnly
        strTitle = "Can't open form"
        MsgBox strMsg, intStyle, strTitle
        Cancel = -1
        DoCmd.Close
    End If
End Sub
```

Items

The Items form (Figure A 14) is used to enter new items or to view existing item details. The search for an item details can be performed by selecting a search field such as ID, Title, Description, Category etc, entering the search text and pressing the search button. Select All button selects all items in the Item table. The form contains three sub forms Authors, Actors and Artists to display item authors if an item is a book, Actors if an item is a DVD and Artists if an item is a CD.

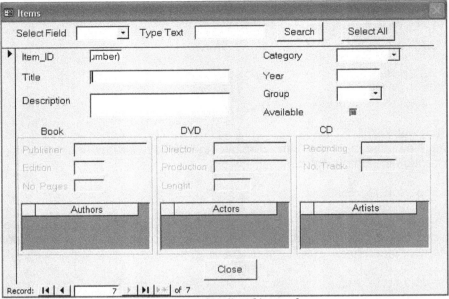

Figure A 14 details of items form

Record source: Items table.

The code that handles the search is the same as the one used in Member form shown earlier in this section. The only difference in code is name of the form. The Items form enables users to input or view items that belong to three different groups: Books, DVDs and CDs. The code listed below controls the display of item details according to the group that they belong to.

This code is attached to the OnCurrent event of the form enables or disables an item specific sections on the form according to the value of the Group attribute.

```
Private Sub Form_Current()
    'Enables or disables item specific sections
    If Me![Group] = 1 Then
        disableDVD_CD
      ElseIf Me![Group] = 3 Then
        disableBook_CD
      ElseIf Me![Group] = 2 Then
        disableBook_DVD
      ElseIf Me![Group] = 0 Then
        disableAll
      End If

End Sub
```

The code below is attached to the OnAfterUpdate event of the Item form and it sets the Available attribute to "Yes" and calls a subroutine, which enables or disables item sections on the form according to the value of the Group attribute. It also moves the focus to the enabled section.

```
Private Sub Group_AfterUpdate()
        'Sets a new Item's field Available to Yes
        Me![Available] = "Yes"
     'Sets the focus to the item specific section according to
    the item group
        If Me![Group] = 1 And IsNull(Publisher) = True Then
```

```
            disableDVD_CD
            DoCmd.GoToControl "Publisher"

        ElseIf Me![Group] = 2 And IsNull(Recording) = True Then
            disableBook_DVD
            DoCmd.GoToControl "Recording"

        ElseIf Me![Group] = 3 And IsNull(Director) = True Then
            disableBook_CD
            DoCmd.GoToControl "Director"

      End If
   End Sub
```

These subroutines enable or disable individual fields for each item specific section.

```
        Private Sub disableDVD_CD()
            'Enables Book section and disables DVD and CD sections
            Form_Items.Publisher.Enabled = True
            Form_Items.Edition.Enabled = True
            Form_Items.Num_of_pages.Enabled = True

            Form_Items.Director.Enabled = False
            Form_Items.Production.Enabled = False
            Form_Items.Lenght.Enabled = False

            Form_Items.Recording.Enabled = False
            Form_Items.Num_of_Tracks.Enabled = False

        End Sub

        Private Sub disableBook_CD()
            'Enables DVD section and disables Book and CD sections
            Form_Items.Publisher.Enabled = False
            Form_Items.Edition.Enabled = False
            Form_Items.Num_of_pages.Enabled = False

            Form_Items.Director.Enabled = True
            Form_Items.Production.Enabled = True
            Form_Items.Lenght.Enabled = True

            Form_Items.Recording.Enabled = False
            Form_Items.Num_of_Tracks.Enabled = False

        End Sub

        Private Sub disableBook_DVD()
            'Enables CD section and disables Book and DVD sections
            Form_Items.Publisher.Enabled = False
            Form_Items.Edition.Enabled = False
            Form_Items.Num_of_pages.Enabled = False

            Form_Items.Director.Enabled = False
            Form_Items.Production.Enabled = False
            Form_Items.Lenght.Enabled = False
```

```
            Form_Items.Recording.Enabled = True
            Form_Items.Num_of_Tracks.Enabled = True

     End Sub

     Private Sub disableAll()
            'Disables all
            Form_Items.Publisher.Enabled = False
            Form_Items.Edition.Enabled = False
            Form_Items.Num_of_pages.Enabled = False

            Form_Items.Director.Enabled = False
            Form_Items.Production.Enabled = False
            Form_Items.Lenght.Enabled = False

            Form_Items.Recording.Enabled = False
            Form_Items.Num_of_Tracks.Enabled = False

     End Sub
```

The sub forms Authors, Actors and Artists on the parent form Items have the same code in their OnDoubleClick even. The code checks if the name of an author, actor or artist exists on their lists and if not enables users to add new author, actor or artist to their tables by double clicking on the corresponding sub form The Author sub form code example is shown below.

```
     Private Sub AuthorID_DblClick(Cancel As Integer)
     On Error GoTo Err_AuthorID_DblClick

          Dim lngAuthorID As Long
          'Check if author exists
          If IsNull(Me![AuthorID]) Then
               Me![AuthorID].Text = ""
          Else
               lngAuthorID = Me![AuthorID]
               Me![AuthorID] = Null
          End If
          'Check if the parent form is loaded
          If IsLoaded("Items") Then
          DoCmd.OpenForm "Authors", , , , , acDialog, "GotoNew"
          End If

          Me![AuthorID].Requery
          If lngAuthorID <> 0 Then Me![AuthorID] = lngAuthorID

     Exit_AuthorID_DblClick:
          Exit Sub

     Err_AuthorID_DblClick:
          MsgBox Err.Description
          Resume Exit_AuthorID_DblClick
     End Sub

     Private Sub AuthorID_NotInList(NewData As String, Response
     As Integer)
```

```
        MsgBox "Double-click this field to add an entry to the
    list."
        Response = acDataErrContinue

    End Sub
```

The variable lngAuthorID and form control AuthorID are replaced with the lngActorID and ActorID in the Actor sub form and lngArtistID and ArtistID in the Artist sub form.

ItemSearch

The ItemSearch form (Figure A 15) provides search features to a member who wishes to search for a specific item and item availability.

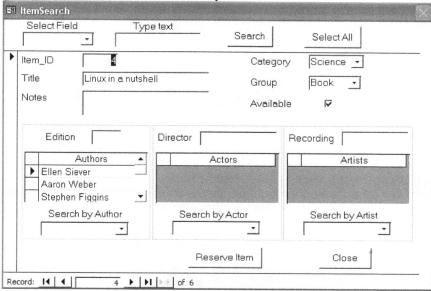

Figure A 15 Details of item search form

The search can be done by an Item ID, Title, Description, Category, Director, or by Author, Actor and Artist. All controls on this form are locked to prevent an accidental data loss. The Booking form can be accessed from this form by pressing the Reserve Item button.

Record sources: Tables Item, Authors, Actors and Artists.

The code that handles the search by Item ID, Title, Description, etc is the same like one used in Member form shown earlier in this section. The only difference in code is name of the form. The code that handles the search by Author, Actor and Artist is shown below. Because the code is the same for all three-combo boxes only search by actor is listed.

The code is attached to the AfterUpdate event of the Actors combo box. If the box is empty all the items from the Item table are selected. If it is not empty only the items that match the Actor ID are selected.

```
        Private Sub cboActorSrch_AfterUpdate()

         Dim strSQL As String

        If IsNull(Me.cboActorSrch) Then
            ' If the combo is Null, use the whole table as the
        RecordSource.
            Me.RecordSource = "Items"
        Else
            strSQL = "SELECT DISTINCTROW Item.* FROM Item " & _
```

```
            "INNER JOIN ActorLines ON " & _
            "Item.Item_ID = ActorLines.Item_ID " & _
            "WHERE ActorLines.Actor_ID = " & Me.cboActorSrch &
";"
        Me.RecordSource = strSQL
    End If

    End Sub
```

This code is attached to the OnGotFocus event of the combo box. When the box gets the focus the other boxes are cleared.

```
        Private Sub cboActorSrch_GotFocus()

          cboAuthorSrch = ""
          cboArtistSrch = ""
          SearchCriteria = ""
          cboSearchField = ""
          txtSearchString = ""

        End Sub
```

Booking

The Booking form (Figure A 16) is used to book an item if one is not available at the time. This form can be accessed through the ItemSearch form only because it is synchronised with the ItemSearch form through the Item ID attribute.

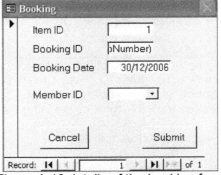

Figure A 16 details of the booking form

To ensure that this form cannot be opened independently the following code is attached to the OnOpen event of the form.

```
        Private Sub Form_Open(Cancel As Integer)
            Dim strMsg As String
            Dim strTitle As String
            Dim intStyle As Integer
            Dim strFName As String
            Dim strCForm As String
            strFName = "BorrowReturn"
            strCForm = Me.Form.Name
            'Check if the parent form is loaded
            If IsLoaded(strFName) Then

        Exit Sub
```

```
                'If the parent form is not loaded display massage and
        cancel opening
            Else
                strMsg = "You cannot open" & " " & strCForm & " " &
        "as a standalone form." & vbCrLf            & _ "It can be
        accessed from" & " " & strFName & " form"
                    intStyle = vbOKOnly
                strTitle = "Can't open form"
                MsgBox strMsg, intStyle, strTitle
                Cancel = -1
                DoCmd.Close
            End If
        End Sub
```

BorrowReturn

The BorrowReturn form (Figure A 17) is used to perform various tasks such as checking a member's current item borrowing details, checking if a member has got any items that are overdue, generating new borrowing sessions, updating an item return details and managing payments for item overdue charges. The CurrentBorrowing sub form shows the current borrowing status of the selected member and the Overdue sub form shows if any of the items currently borrowed by the selected member are overdue. A new borrowing session can be generated by pressing the New Borrowing button, which will open the Borrowing form. An Item return can be generated by pressing the Item Return button, which will open the Return form. Any item overdue charges can be handled by pressing the Payment button, which will open the Payment form.

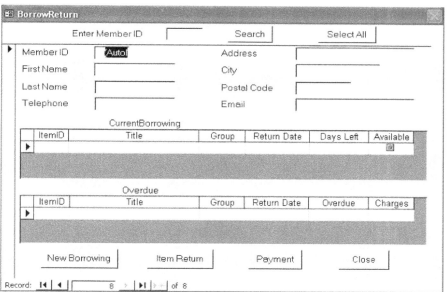

Figure A 17 Details of the borrow and return form

Record source: Member table, CurrentBorrowing query and OverduebyMember query.

The search for the member is handled with the following code.

```
        Private Sub cmdSearch_Click()
        On Error GoTo Err_cmdSearch_Click

            Dim LSQL  As String
            Dim LSearchString As String
            'Check if the textbox is empty
```

117

```
        If Len(IdSearch) = 0 Or IsNull(IdSearch) = True Then
            MsgBox "You must enter a search string."

        Else
            'Filter records by Member ID
            LSearchString = IdSearch

            LSQL = "select * from Member"
            LSQL = LSQL & " where Member_ID LIKE '*" &
LSearchString & "*'"

            Form_BorrowReturn.RecordSource = LSQL

            IdSearch = ""

            MsgBox "Results have been filtered."

        End If

    Exit_cmdSearch_Click:
        Exit Sub

    Err_cmdSearch_Click:
        MsgBox Err.Description
        Resume Exit_cmdSearch_Click

    End Sub
```

Borrowing

The Borrowing form (Figure A 18) is used to generate a new borrowing session. This form is synchronised with the BorrowReturn form through the Member ID attribute and can be opened through the BorrowReturn form only. The child form BorrowLineSub handles a multiple item loans in one session. The child form is linked to the parent form through the Borrowing ID. If any borrowed items have been previously booked they can be cleared from the booking list by pressing the ClearBooked button which will open the ClearBookedItems form.

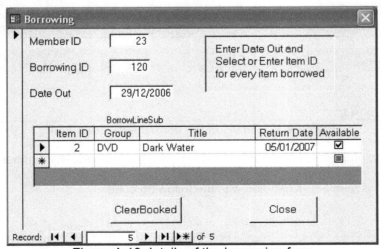

Figure A 18 details of the borrowing form
Record source: Tables Borrowing and Borrow_Line.

To ensure that this form cannot be opened as a standalone form the following code is attached to the OnOpen event of the form.

```
Private Sub Form_Open(Cancel As Integer)

Dim strMsg As String
Dim strTitle As String
Dim intStyle As Integer
Dim strFName As String
Dim strCForm As String

    strFName = "BorrowReturn"
    strCForm = Me.Form.Name

    If IsLoaded(strFName) Then

Exit Sub

    Else
        strMsg = "You cannot open" & " " & strCForm & " " &
"as a standalone form." & vbCrLf & _
        "It can be accessed from the" & " " & strFName & "
form"

        intStyle = vbOKOnly
        strTitle = "Can't open form"
        MsgBox strMsg, intStyle, strTitle
        Cancel = -1
        DoCmd.Close
    End If
End Sub
```

The Due_Date and Available attributes are used dynamically in queries and it is important to update these fields every time an item is borrowed or returned. The following code automatically sets the return date and the Available attribute to "No".

```
Private Sub Item_ID_AfterUpdate()
    'Automatically set the return date
    If Me![Group] = 1 Then
        Me![Due_Date] = [Forms]![Borrowing]![Date_Out] + 14
    Else
        Me![Due_Date] = [Forms]![Borrowing]![Date_Out] + 7
    End If
    'Set the attribute Available to No
    Me![Available] = "No"

End Sub
```

Return

The Return form (Figure A 19) is used to update return details stored in the Borrow_Line table and to set the returned item's available attribute to "Yes". It is very important to update these details because they are used to generate some queries and reports. The Returned attribute from the Borrow_Line table and the Available attribute from the Item table will be automatically set to "Yes" when the Date Returned field has been updated. The form is synchronised with the BorrowReturn form through the Member ID attribute and can be opened through the BorrowReturn form only.

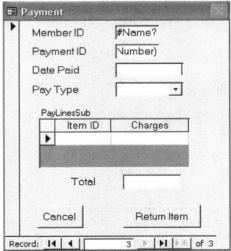

Figure A 19 details of the item return form

Record source: NotReturnedAll query.

To ensure that this form cannot be opened as a standalone form the same code like one used for the Borrowing form above is attached to the OnOpen event. To automatically set the Available and Returned attributes to "Yes" the following code is attached to the BeforeUpdate event.

```
Private Sub Date_Returned_BeforeUpdate(Cancel As Integer)

    Me![Available] = "Yes"
    Me![Returned] = "Yes"


End Sub
```

Payment

The Payment form (Figure A 20) is used to make records of payments for item overdue charges. The form is synchronised with the BorrowReturn form through the Member ID attribute and can be opened through the BorrowReturn form only. Once the payment has been done the item or items can be returned by pressing the Return button, which will open the Return form.

Figure A 20 details of payment form

Record source: Tables Payment and PayLines.

To ensure that this form cannot be opened as a standalone form the same code that was used for the Borrowing form and Return form is attached to the OnOpen event.

The record source for the Item ID combo box on the PayLines sub form is the OverduebyMember query. Because the Payment form is synchronised with the BorrowReturn form the Item ID combo box will list only the overdue items that were borrowed by the member that is currently selected on the BorrowReturn form. Once the overdue item is selected from the combo box the charges for that item will automatically inserted into the Charges field. The following code ensures that charges are inserted.

```
Private Sub Item_ID_AfterUpdate()
  Me![Charges] = Me![Item_ID].Column(2)
End Sub
```

If there are multiple item charges the total is displayed in the Total field.

Employee

The Employee form (Figure A 21) is used to view, edit or add the library employees.

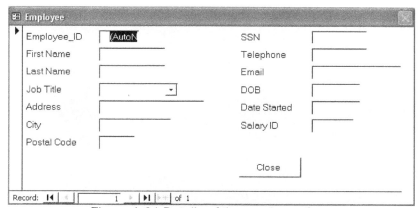

Figure A 21 Details of the employee form

Record source: Employee table.

Salary

The Salary form (Figure A 22) is used to store salary details for each employee.

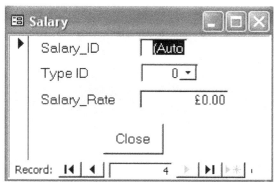

Figure A 22 details of the salary form

Record source: Salary table

Salary Type

The SalaryType form (Figure A22) is used to view, add or edit salary types, which are used to specify each employee's salary.

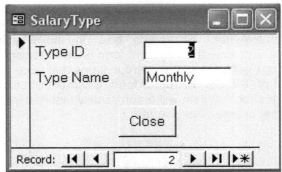
Figure A 22 details of the salary type form

Record source: SalaryType table.

Other forms

The other forms include the Category, Authors, Actors and Artists. All these form share a very similar and simple design. They are used to view, add or edit records. There is no additional code written for these forms.

Record source:

- Category form   ➔   Category table
- Authors form   ➔   Author table
- Actors form   ➔   Actor table
- Artists form   ➔   Artist table

Because of the simplicity of these forms only one example is shown in Figure A 23.

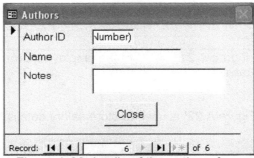
Figure A 23 details of the authors form

TESTING PLAN

This list explains which tests should be carried out once the solution has been developed. The test results will be shown at the end of this section of the report.

Data Input

1. Enter details into the Enrolment form.
Aim: To input the new member details into the Enrolment form and check if they show up on the NewMember sub form.
Expected outcome: The newly entered details should be displayed on the NewMember sub form on the Member form.

2. Update a new member details and activate the membership.
Aim: To update a new member details picked up from the NewMember sub form on the Member form and to activate the membership.

Expected outcome: The new membership is activated and the member's details should be saved in the Member table and cleared from the NewMember sub form.

3. Input a new item.
   Aim: To input a new item details through the Item form.
   Expected outcome: The new item details should be saved in the Item table.

4. Input a new employee.
   Aim: To input a new employee details through the Employee form.
   Expected outcome: The new employee details should be saved in the Employee table.

Item borrowing and returning sessions

1. Generate a new borrowing.
   Aim: To input a new item borrowing details through the BorrowReturn and Borrowing forms.
   Expected outcome: The new generated borrowing details should be displayed in the CurrentBorrowing sub form on the BorrowReturn form and the details should be saved in the Borrowing and Borrow_Line tables. Also the item details should be listed in the CurrentBorrowing report.

2. Generate an item return.
   Aim: To input an item return details through the BorrowReturn and Return forms.
   Expected outcome: The borrowing details for returned item should be updated in the Borrowing and Borrow_Line tables and the item's details should be removed from the CurrentBorrowing sub form on the BorrowReturn form. Also the items details should be removed from the CurrentBorrowing report.

3. Simulate an item overdue.
   Aim: To generate a new item borrowing and set the borrowing date and the return date so that the item's loan duration has expired.
   Expected outcome: The new details should be saved in the Borrowing and Borrow_Line tables and the item details and the overdue charges should be displayed on the Overdue sub form on the BorrowReturn form. Also the item's overdue details should be listed in the Overdue report.

Item search and booking

1. Search for an item by the Item ID.
   Aim: To perform a search for an item on the ItemSearch form by choosing the Item ID field from   the combo box and typing an ID number in the text box.
   Expected outcome: The searched item details should be displayed in the item details section of the form.

2. Search for an item by the item's Title.
   Aim: to perform a search for an item on the ItemSearch form by choosing the Title field from the combo box and typing a title in the text box.
   Expected outcome: The searched item details should be displayed in the item details section of the form

3. Search for an item by author's name.
   Aim: To perform a search for an item on the ItemSearch form by choosing the author's name from the Authors combo box.
   Expected outcome: All selected author's items should be selected and available for viewing in the item details section of the form.

4. Booking an item.

Aim: After the search for an item has been performed the attempt will be made to reserve the item through the Booking form.

Expected outcome: When the item is selected and the Reserve button is pressed the Booking form should open displaying the selected item details. After a members ID is entered into the Booking form the booking details should be saved in the Booking table and listed in the Booking report.

A.1.4 Summary

The contents of the appendix have been provided in order for you to see the components that need to be included in the technical report for a database design. This report was produced by Mr. Borislav Benak in accordance with the example specifications covered in Chapter 6 of this text. From this report you will also note that Visual Basic is used and documented as a programming language within MSAccess. It allows you to control the behaviour of objects in your database as well as to use the graphical user interface forms to work with these objects. I have to add that this has been provided only as an example so that you can appreciate the general idea behind producing technical documentation for your database design.

www.ingramcontent.com/pod-product-compliance
Lightning Source LLC
Chambersburg PA
CBHW081226050326
40689CB00016B/3698